ABOUT THE BOOK

"Memoirs of an Entrepreneur" is a revealing insight into corporate America. The book tells the story of a sales executive who climbed the ladder of corporate success only to find frustration with the dog-eat-dog atmosphere and the complete lack of humanity, which pervades many companies today. Longing for freedom from corporate bondage, endless transfers, and a better lifestyle, Miller took the plunge in 1969 to start his own business.

This chronicle reveals the step-by-step process of building a business, from, "notations in a dog eared file kept for sentimental reasons," to a $40 Million a year enterprise. It distills the knowledge and experience of a person who would not settle for whatever comes along. The author tells of mistakes as well as triumphs noting that; "Good judgment is the result of experience which is the result of bad judgment." Written in story book fashion 'Memoirs' is not just another how-to book but rather a fascinating profile of business, marketing, leadership, and entrepreneurship. Chapter Ten is a biographical sketch of Herbert L. Laube, a little known entrepreneur who shaped Miller's business career, and reshaped the entire air conditioning industry.

If you have ever longed to jump out of the rat race and 'be your own person' this book should be included in your planning kit.

www.memoirs-of-an-entrepreneur.com

MEMOIRS

OF AN

ENTREPRENEUR

How to Escape Corporate Bondage

By Harold Miller

To **Maria Carbonaro**: Assistant Editor of ***The Central New York Business Journal*** who gave readily of her enthusiastic help and support for the writing of this book.

MCS Publishing Company

Cover Design by **coburndesign.com**
Book Design by Henry Kremers

Printed in the United States of America

Memoirs of an Entrepreneur

Introduction

Today's corporate world is largely devoid of any loyalty between employer and employee. In my generation it was not uncommon to join a company right out of school and retire from that company. We were taught that if you applied yourself and excelled in your job you would be rewarded with pay raises, promotions, and a retirement program for the "golden years."

All of this is gone with the wind – of corporate greed, merger mania, and simple survival. In these tumultuous and fast-changing times – compensation, benefits, and retirement programs are as good as the current financial condition and integrity of the owners. When the small, privately owned company that I worked for was sold to a large conglomerate in 1966, my future was placed in the hands of a group of people, in New York City, who didn't even know where Auburn, New York was on the map. They had not the slightest understanding of our business nor did they appreciate the dedicated employees who built it. Commitments made by the previous owner soon were broken, and compensation programs – tied to the growth of our business – evaporated. It soon became painfully clear that the only person in that organization who was interested in my future – was me.

So what to do about it? Going to work for another company was an alternative, but with no guarantee the same thing would not happen again. A better alternative would be to start my own business, and be free of corporate bondage for good. As sales manager, I certainly knew how to sell their products, but how do you parley this into a business? With a young and growing family, our bank account was pretty thin, and many questions emerged – such as financing the venture, finding the right people, and even the structure of the business itself. The statistics of success are daunting, only one of five businesses survives beyond two years. The answer to these questions, and many others, is the subject of this chronicle.

Since there are literally thousands of "how to" books on the shelves, why is this one unique? Well — they say that good judgment is the result of experience, which is the result of bad judgment. Our miss-calls were almost as important as the right ones in forming the fabric of our emerging companies. Both are revealed herein.

Scratch a businessman, or an entrepreneur, and you will likely find a salesman. Salesmen are born with unique DNA, but training is still necessary to sharpen skills, and therefore the art of selling is explored in detail.

The prime business we chose was to be an independent manufacturer's representative – which is a highly insecure business, and yet offers great rewards for those willing to take the gamble. As the business became successful, we invested some of our earnings in outside ventures, such as real estate and development, in order to 'copper our bets' – as the saying goes. I then graduated to the ranks of an entrepreneur.

If you have the itch to break free from the stifling atmosphere of the corporation, to be your own person – if you want to avoid being a victim of circumstances – if you long to enjoy the personal and financial freedom of running your own show, and living life as you choose – read on.

Foreword

Most people who climb the ladder of success have a mentor – someone who recognizes their ability, and shepherds their development. My mentor was Herbert Livingston Laube – to whom this book is dedicated. Herb defined everything that is a leader, industrialist, businessman, and entrepreneur. Very simply, he taught me everything I know about how to operate a business. His amazing story is revealed in Chapter Ten.

Laube was Vice President of Engineering for Carrier Corporation in the 1940s. He became a rebel within the air conditioning industry, and would come to have a significant influence on its future direction.

Herb was in line to become president of Carrier Corporation, but had a falling out with President Cloud Wampler, regarding product and market development for the burgeoning commercial air conditioning market that began after WWII. Herb believed that Carrier should develop decentralized air conditioning systems that he discovered were more efficient than chiller based central plants. Willis Carrier had invented the chiller, and Wampler was afraid that the system Laube was pursuing would cannibalize their chiller sales, and so he killed the idea.

The resultant frustration caused Laube to resign from Carrier in 1948 to form his own company, which he named Remington Air Conditioning Division. His company would go on to introduce energy conservation to the air conditioning industry, and Laube became the father of what is known as 'green buildings' today.

I went to work for Remington in 1961 and soon became sales manager. At that time, unbeknownst to me, the company was close to bankruptcy. However, due to Laube's dedication, and the hard work of his equally dedicated management team, Remington returned to financial health a few years later. All this took its toll on Herb, and he sold the business to Singer Company in 1966. Singer was becoming a conglomerate – it was all the rage at that time. I will never completely understand what causes companies to exceed their grasp, and acquire businesses for which they have little or no knowledge or understanding. None of the major conglomerates that existed at that time have survived intact today. Having failed to learn the lessons of the 1970s, the big corporations are at it again – ignoring the economic and human upheaval they create – fueled by ego and greed.

Edward Wasserman, former editor of the *Daily Business Review*, hit the nail on the head when he wrote: "U.S. industry buys and sells itself cyclically, puffing up and blowing out. The economic rationale is as predictable as a moonrise. When everyone is bulking up, it's to profit from synergies and scale, when everybody's selling it's to rededicate to their core business and unlock shareholder value. The economics is often bogus. Most mergers don't work and most divestitures are mere preludes to other mergers."

Singer's takeover of Remington Air Conditioning produced frustration for Herb Laube, and those of us who helped build the company. After dealing with a parade of 'experts' from the home office – who tried to run our company like a sewing machine manufacturer – I resigned in 1968 to start my own business – never looking back.

CHAPTER ONE

Corporate Life

"It's the best game I'd ever seen."

I joined Remington in 1961 as regional sales manager. It was a privately owned business and Herb Laube was president and chief executive officer. Actually, he was the whole show, being all-at-once the director of marketing, engineering, and manufacturing – even writing the advertising literature. I learned much from this man, who handpicked his key people, and became everyone's mentor – everyone that is whom he deemed to be potentially successful in their respective positions. He drove himself and those around him relentlessly. Those who could not stand the heat – soon evacuated the kitchen. The result was a small but effective management group who carved new markets within the air conditioning industry.

Unknown to me, Remington was deeply in debt. In 1954 they had shipped hundreds of air conditioners to their distributors on open credit, but a recession developed that year, and their distributors had unsold inventory in their warehouses. The distributors could not pay Remington, and in turn Remington could not pay their suppliers. This created a chain reaction that put the company deeply in debt. Laube could have declared bankruptcy and opened a new business across the street (per our government-sponsored "surgical bankruptcy" of General Motors in 2009), but this would be a violation of his principles. Instead, he contacted all of his suppliers and pledged that Remington would pay all debts, with interest.

It took several years and a lot of hard work, but it was accomplished. However, Remington's success and growth produced its own problems and Herb – stressed by the entire scenario – decided that it was time to step aside. That time came in 1966. Laube realized that it would take a large infusion of capital to expand manufacturing facilities to accommodate increased sales. He was deeply committed to the principle of decentralized energy conservation air conditioning, but realized that he could not capture the potential market without financial backing and manufacturing expertise.

One day Laube announced to his staff that we would be 'merging' with Singer Company. We were soon to learn that with every merger there is a sub-merge. When Mercedes Benz was courting Chrysler Corporation the pitch was "a merger of equals." Afterwards, Jurgen Schrempp, who became CEO of Daimler Chrysler, admitted that they never had any such intention. After years of frustration by all parties involved, Mercedes sold Chrysler and, like a lady of the night, Chrysler has been passed off from one company to another since then.

When Singer Corporation was wooing Remington Air Conditioning, the party line was, "Nothing will change – Remington people will continue to run the business, Singer will supply the capital for expansion, and lend their manufacturing expertise." This too, was just a pitch to keep the troops from jumping ship. Herb Laube, who founded the business, became a 'consultant' – and by his own definition – a "castrated tomcat."

His gracious office was only slightly smaller than the new general manager's next door, but nobody came to see him because he was a lame duck. Herb, later reflecting upon the situation, said, "This was the biggest mistake I ever made – hell – I wasn't satisfied with the way I ran the business much less waiting around to see someone else screw things up."

 He didn't last long.

Soon, we were exposed to working for a large corporation. It is much like working for the government – layer upon layer of supervisors, managers and departments. Decisions became agonizing lengthy transactions with enough reports and market analysis to choke a horse. Empire building is a fact of corporate life. It works like this – the more staff you have working under you, the more important you are and the more the company needs you to sort out the staff you have created. Life in a large corporation is very much depersonalized. We never met most of the heads of the many departments our small sales group reported to – much less David Kircher, the President of Singer Corporation. One day, the head of all manufacturing for Singer came to our plant in Auburn, New York. He gathered the management staff together and announced, "We know you have manufacturing problems up here in *Albany* [confused about where he was], and I'm here to help you."

I was soon promoted to National Sales Manager of Singer/Remington and was transferred to Singer headquarters at Rockefeller Center in New York City. Working in this kind of environment was something to behold. As businessman Robert Shapiro – who dumped a large corporation to start his own business and likewise wrote a book about it – said, "It's the best game I'd ever seen."

The first lessons to be learned by anyone wishing to climb the ladder of success are the rungs of status. My office was on the 63rd floor overlooking Central Park (status one) with a closet, drapes, carpet, couch, and water closet (status two through five). This raised many eyebrows because my office was well above the status of a 'salesman' in Singer's parlance. After all, in Singer's hierarchy, a salesman was just a glorified clerk who sold sewing machines and accessories in Singer's many retail stores around the country.

Then I ran smack-dab into the New York City 'attitude' that can best be described as arrogant ignorance. There is a poster that hangs on the wall of many shops and offices in NYC which depicts the Manhattan skyline with the Hudson River in the background – shortly beyond is the Golden Gate Bridge in San Francisco. The title is, "A New Yorkers View of America." There is more truth than humor in this artful depiction. Most New Yorkers believe that anyone living in the "flyover zone" beyond the George Washington Bridge and the West Coast resides in a doublewide trailer and milks cows for a living. Moreover, any idea that does not emanate from that slab of rock between the East River and the Hudson River, is not worth a damn.

Singer ran our business 'by the numbers' and they were in love with five-year plans. We were to double and redouble our sales within five years. I was given the green light to hire four new regional sales managers immediately. When I asked how we would find these key people so quickly, the new general manager – a Singer transplant from the 'Big Apple' – dismissively said, "That's your problem."

The hooker in this rapid expansion plan was that our profits had to keep pace with their investment, and a large share of our profits went to support the mother church for management and administrative fees. If we failed to 'make the numbers' then we must scale back proportionately. This syndrome became known as "Black Fridays" (the last weekly business day of quarterly financial reporting periods). All this produced a constant pressure-cooker atmosphere and caused many to overreact. The chickens came home to roost in December of 1967 – a little over a year from the time Singer took over. I had hired a regional manager for the Southwest (a territory where we had no previous sales presence). Jake Johnson was experienced in sales management, but it was necessary to build sales from scratch plus find and train manufacturers' representatives.

Even Superman could not have produced results in the few months Jake was aboard. Nonetheless, "Black Fridays" worked on a last-in-first-out basis and we had missed the profit numbers for the year and Jake had to go. The week before Christmas I flew to Dallas to give Jake his Christmas present. It was a heart-rending experience that caused me to completely lose any enthusiasm for the dog-eat-dog corporate life.

A year later, ironically at Christmas time, the final straw came. Singer had transplanted a new general manager from headquarters in NYC. Stuart Tisdale was the epitome of corporate charm and charisma – young and handsome with steely blue eyes and impeccable personal credentials. He had been a tank commander during WWII and thereafter played football for the Pittsburgh Steelers.

His corporate credentials were equally impressive, with a dossier that included bailing out a sick manufacturing plant that Singer operated in Maine. Stu had two families with five children from his first marriage, and five with his second wife. Family number two was moved to Auburn when he was transferred, and he spent every other weekend with wife and family number one in Maine. Stu commuted back and forth in his Beechcraft Bonanza, which was kept at Skaneateles airdrome near the factory.

He was a dynamic guy – but he possessed not one wit of knowledge about the air conditioning business and he had a drinking problem (that was undoubtedly brought on by the pressured life he found himself trapped in). I liked Stu and we got along fine until he called me into his office on the Friday before Christmas and announced that I would be reporting to a new general sales manager who had previously been product manager.

Jim Bennett had been hired by Herb Laube as regional manager and promoted to product manager by Singer when I was promoted to sales manager. We worked on a parallel basis and clashed over everything from product development to literature. Jim was a procrastinator and had a hard time making decisions. It took him six months to make a decision on the cover art for a new product catalogue that our field salesman desperately needed. We disagreed on just about everything and I could never work under him. After carefully explaining this to Stu I asked him to think about it for the weekend.

He agreed.

After leaving our meeting it occurred to me that, for all practical purposes, I had quit. Tisdale would never reverse his decision because it would be contrary to his – and Singer's – management creed. What would I do for a living? Getting another job in sales management would not be a problem because I had been approached several times by competitive manufacturers; however, working for another large corporation was out of the question. Before arriving home that cold December evening – the decision was made.

CHAPTER TWO

Planning the Business

"Plan your work and work your plan"

The thoughts of starting a business had been in the back of my mind ever since being forced to fire Jake Johnson. This example of cold-hearted corporate management is even more prevalent today in the electronic age. Recently, the CEO of a large corporation fired 400 employees via e-mail. This notwithstanding, it was painfully clear to me even back in 1968 – that corporate life was not for me. The crash of 2008 wiped out so many careers (Wall Street took an incredible beating) that it becomes even more evident that having your own business is the only real security

The decision about what to do with my career at this juncture – was made.

If you are contemplating going into business, the first thing to do is to list the pros and cons. The con was obvious. I call it "fear of flying" – which is cutting off that steady paycheck and reaching into your own pocket for your income. What if you become ill? What if you fail? These factors stop most people. It almost stopped me. Without the support of my wife, it could never have happened. Laube had told me, during one of our many extended discussions that the man of the family stokes the furnace, and business decisions were his to make. However, I looked upon our marriage as a lifelong partnership with each partner contributing equally to the success of the family. In any event, it was an academic thought process because in the end, it was my wife who tipped the scales in favor of starting the new business.

The major 'pro' for making this move was to create a better lifestyle and to escape corporate bondage. It is a fact of life that your income will always be controlled working for others. When I was regional manager for Remington, my base salary was augmented by an override based on sales from my region – which was expanding exponentially. When my income became greater than the president of the company, the formula was soon adjusted downward. Then, when Singer took over the company, my income was further reduced because Singer was a manufacturing company and did not compensate its employees based on sales. Given equal talent, effort, and results – a person can always make more money in their own business – particularly in the sales business. Another compelling reason was the fact that I had an inept boss (this probably prompts more people to start their own business than any other factor).

Very close to the criteria for earning a good living was quality of life. During my tenure as sales manager I traveled most of the time and spent time in every major city in the country. My office was in New York City for eighteen months. During this time I experienced life in the big cities which included commuting, traffic jams and pollution – all of which creates a harried life. The only thing that kept me going during the week was looking forward to the weekend and returning to our new home which was recently built on Owasco Lake – one of the Finger Lakes of Central New York. I began to fantasize about being able to return home every night instead of just weekends, to swim mornings before going to my own office, and to be around every day as our kids were growing up.

The second step towards creating a business is – what kind of business. The old adage, "cobbler stick to your last" means staying within the discipline or trade of your field. Avoid the get-rich-quick schemes that are huckstered on TV. If anyone can do it, then what edge do you have for creating a business?

One of Laube's axioms was, "A small company doing business in competition with large companies in the same field – should be unique." The primary tools for business success are mainly, your technical knowledge, management skills, salesmanship, and the one ingredient that stops most people – focused effort. I had approached one of my contemporaries at Singer about going into business with me. He told me bluntly, "It's not for me – I'm not cut out for sleeping under the desk and eating peanut butter sandwiches for lunch."

Thomas J. Watson, the legendary founder of IBM said, "Plan your work and work your plan." I say, "Plan your business and then work your plan." Hanging out a shingle is not enough. If you do not draft a roadmap, it is next to impossible to reach your goal. The following steps constitute a tried and true method of getting where you want to go. Over the weekend, the plan was put together that encompassed the basic elements of starting the new business. That plan, scribbled on a pad and placed in a dog-eared file, exists to this day – for sentimental reasons. Every once in a while I open that dog-eared file to see if we're staying on track.

Financing – This is the first and most crucial step towards starting a business. Everything else flows from this piece of the puzzle. Hardly anyone working for a company in a middle management position is able to save enough to start a business – depending on its nature. Bank financing may be necessary. Fortunately, our intended venture was similar to being a broker, so that our basic need was an office and business machines. Today, it would be far more expensive in the electronic age.

Singer Company 'bankrolled' some of their reps by advancing money based on a draw against future commissions. I was confident that we could secure a similar arrangement – which we did. Added to this was the grand sum of $2,500 withdrawn from our thin bank account. Alternate methods of financing would include a second mortgage on your house, a rich uncle, or selling an interest in the business – none of which I would recommend.

The bottom line is, if you do not have sufficient financing, and if you cannot generate enough income and profits to cover debt service, payroll, and expenses right from the get-go, your new business is in jeopardy. Most new businesses fail for lack of proper financing.

Personnel – Getting the right people will be your most daunting challenge. This is where we had a real edge having worked with many sharp young guys within Singer/Remington's ranks. I had developed several close personal relationships during my tenure at Singer/Remington and hoped to cash in on this advantage (see Chapter Five, The Dream Team).

Actually, our approach was not unique. Herb Laube incorporated many ex-Carrier people into his staff when he founded Remington. As a matter of fact, it is almost standard operating procedure. When the CEO of a corporation splits with his employer, he usually pirates some of his 'team' into his next business venture. This becomes a corporate double-edged sword as the law of physics dictates that 'two objects cannot occupy the same space.' Heads have to roll to make room for the transplanted staff. If a person does not have the luxury of enticing known quantities into their new business venture, then the task of recruiting good people is usually more difficult. On the other hand, there are many good people out there who are as frustrated with corporate bondage as I was. If you plan to be a one-man-show then there is no staffing problem (refer back to sleeping under the desk and eating peanut butter sandwiches for lunch).

Office facilities – Today there is much emphasis on home offices, but I contend that few businesses can be successfully operated out of the home. There is too much temptation for the wife to say; "Honey, watch the kids while I go to the store." If your child falls and skins a knee, even though you are engaged in negotiating an order you'll have to say, "Let me call you back." Even if you don't have family members at home there are just too many potential distractions for you to fully concentrate.

I had an office in our home for six years while working for Hal Walsh (see Epilogue Part One - page 92) and I can attest to the problems. Successful business people need to maintain an atmosphere where serious business can be conducted. Professionals need to surround themselves with the trappings of a successful business. Your office should be the showcase of your company, regardless of size, and it should be used to attract customers, clients, and employees.

Accounting facilities – A businessman who keeps his own books has a fool for a client. In the complicated realm of finance, taxes and accounting, only the experts can thread their way through the maze. Accountants and lawyers rule the business world – they have cleverly planned it that way. One of your first priorities should be to hook up with a tax consultant. They can do your tax returns, guide you in setting up the business, and pay their way by saving tax dollars. An ad in the Help Wanted column will locate someone to keep the books on a part time basis, in the beginning. You should never waste time doing menial office work – it is a waste of your talent. The way to become big is to think big.

Legal facilities – The first thing that anyone should do when starting a business is to contact a lawyer. The company should be incorporated to protect your personal assets, plus myriad other potential liabilities. Doing business in today's increasingly litigious society is like walking through a financial minefield. We were never involved in a lawsuit for the first 25 years but then we were sued for selling a piece of equipment that leaked water on a mainframe computer. Our company did not manufacture the product, nor did we install it, but nonetheless, we got caught up in the 'deep pockets' strategy so prevalently used today – which is sue everyone in sight and hope to collect from someone who doesn't have a lawyer or doesn't want to waste time in court.

As our businesses became more complex it became necessary to have non-compete contracts drawn up with key people and recently our companies have had to contract with a human resources consultant (HRC) to protect us from lawsuits caused by our having to terminate employees. You can no longer fire people today just because they are incompetent or lazy. For all these reasons and more, every proprietor should consider legal consultation to be a vital tool for conducting business.

Trade Announcements – The best advertisements are usually free. A press release sent to the trade journals and to the local newspapers serving your area of operation is usually very effective. The best trade announcement, however, will be a personal letter with your 'mission statement' sent to all prospective clients and customers (see Chapter Four).

Our business would start with a telephone, a typewriter, and a copy machine. Obviously the start-up cost is much greater today with the advent of computers and other sophisticated office machinery. My mother – a retired accountant – was pressed into service to set up the books and my wife became secretary. While a new business venture has obstacles to overcome, it also has an advantage over established operations. Most people are attracted to new businesses. There is a soft spot for the little guy struggling against the establishment. Another motivating factor for potential customers is the attraction of a new source of supply in order to keep the competition on their toes. The problem will not be getting orders – it will be how you perform when something goes wrong – and inevitably things will go wrong.

CHAPTER THREE

Fear of Flying

"Why don't you do it anyway?"

After spending the weekend polishing the plan to build a business around the considerable experience gained from traveling the country and working with some of the finest independent manufacturers' representatives in the air conditioning industry – a feeling of confidence arose. True – there were potential drawbacks – Carrier Corporation's world headquarters was in Syracuse and the huge sign on the Thompson Road Plant, which read, "The World's Number One Air Conditioning Maker," would be a constant reminder of its local political and economical strength. However, my strategy would be to specialize in decentralized energy conservation air conditioning systems – a concept that Carrier never believed in and did not promote.

These thoughts went through my mind as I drove to the office Monday morning. I met with general manager Stu Tisdale the first thing. There was no doubt that he would approve the plan to become a manufacturer's representative for Singer/Remington products in Upstate New York. Tisdale called Jim Bennett into the office and presented the proposal. Bennett was so happy to get me out of his hair that he jumped at the idea. In effect I would still be working for them as an independent salesman. All agreed, providing that I remain as field sales manager through the first quarter of 1969 in order to help find and train a replacement.

Discipline and character were sorely tested over the next few months as I buried myself in the business at hand. Thoughts of the new venture had to be relegated for off-hours. We were able to find a recruit for sales manager from the ranks of Chrysler-Airtemp, a competitive air conditioning manufacturer. Ray Setimo was their sales manager and like me had reached the end of the line with the company he worked for. Unlike me, Ray decided to stay with a corporation (ironically, after a short stint with

Singer, and after being caught up in a 'Black Friday,' Setimo became Singer/Remington's representative in Buffalo, New York).

During those first three months of 1969, I traveled the country, signing up new representatives, and holding sales meetings from coast-to-coast. In late January, Singer/Remington's management staff met in Chicago for our industry's annual trade show. Tisdale flew with me back to Syracuse and asked for a ride home from the airport. During our drive he confessed that he had made a mistake by appointing Bennett as sales manager, because Jim had become unpopular with the field sales force.

Stu asked me to stay with the company and said he would, "correct the mistake within six months." This turn of events caused the fear of flying to emerge. To stay meant a good income and tenure with one of the largest company's in the industry. Our fifth child had been born just a year earlier, we had just built a new home, and our bank account had dwindled to nearly nothing. Now, I tried to un-sell my wife on starting the new business in favor of the security of staying with Singer. After what I thought was one of my better sales pitches, she responded with all the reasoning of a loving, caring wife. She said, "Why don't you do it anyway – I know you'll be happier."

Looking back on the momentous decision to leave the security of a major company merely reinforced what a risk it was. Let's face it – the odds are stacked against success. According to the U.S. Small Business Administration, more than half of new businesses fail in the first year. However, once you have made the leap and landed on your feet, the next jump is easier.

I would make the move from businessman to entrepreneur within five years of starting the first business venture. Entrepreneurship is a completely different ballgame – the risks are usually higher, but then so are the rewards. Financing a venture becomes easier once you establish a financial track record. We would run our businesses on a pay-as-you-go basis, but actually one of our financial consultants suggested that we borrow some money in order to establish a credit record – which we never did. When it comes time to borrow money for commercial mortgages, your personal balance sheet is the major factor.

March 15, 1969, was the last day on the job working for Singer Company. After conducting a seminar for the West Coast representatives in Las Vegas – I hopped a plane to Minneapolis in order to sign a contract to represent another manufacturer. If an independent manufacturer's representative wishes to stay independent they do not put all their eggs in one basket.

As the airplane lifted off the runway on that beautiful spring morning, a feeling of peace, happiness and excitement displaced anxiety. My future was in my hands. The anticipation of taking the new business as far as talent, hard work, and imagination could go – was exhilarating. There was not a doubt in my mind that the venture would be successful.

CHAPTER FOUR

The Mission

"Politicians, prostitutes, and ugly buildings get respectable if they last long enough"*

If you follow the plan outlined in Chapter Two, you have a roadmap for building your business. Now it is time to implement it. A good way to start is to draft a 'mission statement' which describes your business to the trade.

This was ours.

Gentlemen;

We are a new firm of air conditioning manufacturers' representatives serving Central New York State. The air conditioning business is spread among many manufacturers, products and systems. Since the field is so diverse we believe there is a need for specialization. Therefore, it is our intention to specialize in the growing field of decentralized, factory assembled, heating and cooling systems for the commercial, institutional and industrial building markets.

The business philosophy of Modular Comfort Systems is really quite simple. We consider ourselves to be *customer* representatives as well as *manufacturers'* representatives. Our customers are the designers and builders of buildings. Our goal is to provide knowledgeable technical assistance, project control accuracy – from order to installation and beyond – as well as prompt, competent service as required. We shall endeavor to represent manufacturers of highest quality products whose business doctrine coincides with ours.

Although this is a new company the principals are not new to this area or to the industry. Our combined experience in engineering, sales, marketing and management spans more than 40 years, most of it spent in Upstate New York.

Very Truly Yours;

Harold S. Miller

*Noah Cross – the crusty old entrepreneur in the movie *Chinatown* made this wry comment about success. The same analogy holds true for any business.

Selling chillers and other central station air conditioning equipment would be daunting in Carrier's backyard. Instead, we would create a new market. Decentralized air conditioning systems, particularly heat pumps, are far more energy efficient, cost less to install, and provide greater comfort for the occupants of multi-room buildings. This indisputable fact launched Remington Air Conditioning Company and it launched Modular Comfort Systems.

Our business began in a small rented office with my mother answering the phone, taking and getting mail from the post office, and keeping the books. Since we had five young children at home my 'secretary' Janet typed the correspondence at home from my dictation into a tape machine – usually while driving the car to and from sales calls. The inertia of start-up requires much more effort in the beginning – much like a train huffing and puffing and spinning its wheels (except we didn't spin our wheels). Our plan was to staff the business with a 'dream team' from Singer/Remington which included bright, young dynamic guys that I had worked with and admired.

We needed to sell several big jobs right away in order to finance the dream team.

The first big break came as a result of knowing the economic facts of life that every developer must know if they plan to make a profit. A New York City developer purchased and planned to renovate a major office building in the heart of downtown Syracuse. The Chimes Building resembled the buildings of Rockefeller Center, which was no accident since renowned architect Raymond Hood designed both buildings. The New York City developer planned to use the same type of air conditioning system used in Rockefeller Center – which was a very costly central plant.

The hitch was that no one could afford to install and operate a Madison Avenue air conditioning system based on Syracuse's rental income rates. Our decentralized system would cost one-third as much to install and one-half as much to operate. Knowing that the developer would scrap the New

York City system when he received the bids, we pre-empted the process by calling him beforehand and explaining the economics, ending the conversation by saying, "When you get your bids, you will realize that you can't get an acceptable return on your investment by utilizing the costly air conditioning system as designed. If you will then give me a call we can obtain a firm bid by a reputable local contractor on a decentralized energy conserving system. This is the system of choice in Syracuse and we can produce several references."

Within a week the developer called and repeated my offer saying, "I am interested to receive that firm bid by a reputable contractor." We got the job, and since there was no competition – made an obscene profit. This launched our company and proved some strategic selling factors. First, 'The Golden Rule' – he who has the gold makes the rule, followed by the prime analogy that all business decisions are usually made for profit, or fear of the loss of profit.

The stars were aligned for the building industry in the early 1970s – shortly after our company began. The first baby boomers – those born when the soldiers returned from WW II – fueled the strongest building boom our country had ever experienced. By then, they were well-educated adults having children of their own. America needed housing, hospitals, schools, office buildings and – as families moved to the suburbs – shopping malls. All these building types were best served by the decentralized, energy conserving, air conditioning systems that we specialized in. Fortunately, the 'Big Three' air conditioning manufacturers (Carrier, Trane and York) were mired in the past, and still promoted traditional central systems. This left the field wide open for us.

The building boom produced a new breed of entrepreneur/developer/ builder. Traditionally, buildings were built to order. An architect was hired, plans were drawn, and bids were taken. This process usually took several months, even years. The new breed of developer/builder saw the need and built on speculation. This gave birth to the design/ build process which drastically reduced the time necessary to build buildings. Very often, the shovel was in the ground before the drawings started. Many times construction led drawings, necessitating 'as built' drawings to record how the building was actually built.

In the construction business – perhaps as no other – time is money. Construction financing at high interest rates is a significant part of development expense. This factor also played into our hands. Traditional central air conditioning equipment was built to order. A custom-made chiller normally took at least 26 weeks to produce from time of order. Decentralized system equipment, such as packaged heat pumps and rooftop packaged air conditioners, were pre-built and often stocked in the manufacturer's warehouse. Therefore, the builder could have his air conditioning equipment on site in four to eight weeks – or less.

We were successful in selling this concept to Robert Congel and Michael Falcone, budding young entrepreneurs, who became a new breed of developer/builder. Upon hearing that they were planning a new office park in suburban Syracuse called "Widewaters," we asked for the opportunity to make a presentation to The Pyramid Company. Sitting in the conference room that day, along with Congel, were other partners including Joe Scudieri and Tom McDonald – all of whom would later form their own independent development companies. The presentation included facts and figures of the estimated owning and operating cost savings, as compared to the traditional central air conditioning plants that they had been using.

Not only did we sell the job, but the ripple effect was also unbelievable. From that time on we practically owned the multi-room building air conditioning market in Upstate New York.

The next step in the evolution of energy conservation and energy management of office buildings and other multi-room buildings (today called 'green buildings') occurred when Mike Falcone's Pioneer Companies developed One Park Place in downtown Syracuse.

Pioneer learned that every dollar saved in the owning and operating cost of a building could be directly utilized to offer lower leasing costs to their prospective clients. New technology emerged in the 1980s which combined computer controlled direct digital temperature control, with the already highly efficient decentralized water source heat pumps to produce the lowest energy consumption. One Park Place set a new standard by lowering the consumption of heat, light, and power by more than 50 percent judged next to any comparable building ever built – setting a new benchmark for all that followed.

Thus our business would be built on – and would flourish on – the age-old axiom of selling benefits not hardware. Show a prospective customer how your goods or services will enhance their profits and you will usually make a sale. We were able to carve a market for energy conserving air conditioning where none existed by implementing this simple business principle.

CHAPTER FIVE

The Dream Team

"Before you have Rabbit stew the first thing
You have to do is catch a Rabbit"

Before we could hire our dream team we had to have the income to support them and that meant – sales. Every business is built on sales, unless it is an eleemosynary (non-profit) organization. Some businesses end up that way, but this should not be your goal. Fortunately, we were able to corner the commercial builder/developer construction market soon after Modular Comfort Systems began in 1969. When the income was on the books – we began the quest to hire the people we knew would help insure our long term success

First on my list of 'bright young guys' was Ron Munn who came to Singer from a small manufacturer of heating equipment in South Bend, Indiana and one of the three small companies – including Remington – acquired by Singer to form the Climate Control Division. We got to know each other by working in parallel sales management jobs. Subsequently, Ron built a home next door to ours on the lake, and our families became close friends. Often we would daydream about starting our own business when the frustration of working for Singer became too great. During the weekend, while I was planning the new business, Ron stopped by the house. He asked what was going on and when I told him about the new business venture being planned he said, "Count me in." Subsequently he would become my partner and, together, we built an enterprise beyond anything imagined at that prophetic moment.

The next person we convinced to join the team was Singer/ Remington's national service manager Lou Rapini. His main attribute was a common sense approach to complex mechanical problems. He also had the ability to get the job done, having been hired, trained, and mentored by Herb Laube.

Next aboard was a product manager who had been service manager before Lou and was another member of Laube's management team. No one knew the products better than Vince Lopez, and although he was not a salesman's salesman, he would win our customer's respect because of his technical knowledge and honest straight-forward approach to engineering sales.

Irene Adams – Laube's former secretary – was the next key member of my dream team. She would be our Gal Friday. Irene was a fire-brand, but her experience and work output was exemplary – she would ruffle a few feathers once in a while, but was worth the trouble.

Some people fell in our lap. One day a key technician from the product development lab showed up looking for a job – another victim of Singer's "Black Fridays." Terry Crane also ruffled feathers and was not too popular with Singer management. He was hired on the spot and became one of our key technicians – still working with us some 40-odd years later. Terry would not say three words if two would suffice, and did not suffer fools gladly. Nonetheless, Terry would become a lynch-pin of our future energy management business.

At this juncture, I was called on the carpet by Singer's general manager, and my former boss Stu Tisdale (no one ever called him Stuart). I pleaded not guilty to pirating some of their key people (well – maybe we were a wee bit guilty), explaining that in most cases the people involved were frustrated and looking for jobs. In any event I agreed not to hire anymore people unless it was with Singer's approval. Actually, the bird was picked clean of those we wanted and could afford to hire, so this pledge was not much of a handicap. With every merger, acquisition, buyout – call it what you will – there is an accompanying attrition of people who are frustrated with the new management group. We merely capitalized on this fact of business life.

Staffing the new business with known quantities was a huge advantage. As the company grew we were forced to hire unknown quantities, and soon learned that the three most useless tools to evaluate a prospective employee were résumés, interviews, and references. First of all, résumés have become such a cliché that their only value seems to be for entertainment purposes. Interviews reveal little about a person's work habits or personal habits, and references have been reduced to merely confirming employment. In today's business world, an employer must walk a tightrope of legal discrimination and mandated benefits. If you make a mistake in judgment it is almost impossible to fire an employee for laziness or even incompetence. Most interviews today revolve around an employee's 'rights' and 'benefits' – the equivalent of the Miranda Act. Consequently it has become necessary for our companies to hire a human resources consultant – *to protect our rights.*

The greatest reluctance in starting the company was whether or not I could manage the business end. On the other hand, I had worked with the best manufacturers' representatives in the country, and they were automatically good businessmen and managers – they had to be in order to survive. We soon learned that it was not necessary to know every aspect, such as accounting, legal and tax issues, it was only necessary to engage those who did. Some companies set up a board of directors in order to steer the ship. We were able to set up a 'brain trust' without impaneling a formal board of directors. For example, a good friend of the family, Horace Landry, was a partner in a local accounting firm and taught accounting at Syracuse University. Another friend, Bob Contiguglia, was a prominent local lawyer, who helped set up our businesses from a legal standpoint.

Your investment in a business encompasses much more than the physical plant, it is also necessary to invest of yourself. Don't expect to hire people, give them a job description, place them on the organization chart, and sit back to watch the profits come in. You must be a mentor to your employees, directing them, motivating them, developing their skills, and keeping them focused.

Failure to be a good proprietor is the number one reason that companies fail. I learned all of this from my mentor Herb Laube – who was the quintessential proprietor, manager, and teacher. He set the pace for others by his example. Herb ran a tight ship. Remington had staff meetings for key people at 7:30 *sharp* every Monday morning. Everything was reviewed including sales, product development, manufacturing, quality control and future planning. If anyone had committed, at a previous meeting, to have a report or some information ready and failed to do so – they had a problem. Herb had an uncanny penchant for smoking out the slackers. Another major reason that companies fail is for lack of leadership, follow-up, and follow-through (see Chapter Eight, The Art of Leadership). Our companies still have staff meetings every Monday morning at 7:30 sharp!

A successful business venture should not only define its mission, but also define its customers, and method of operation. You must learn how to do business the way business is being done. Our primary business was selling energy conserving air conditioning systems and our customers were all involved in the building industry. Moreover, we had decided to sell unique systems and products that flew in the face of convention. In order to be successful, it would be necessary to create a market where none existed. If we were successful, there would be no competition for a time giving us the opportunity to establish a customer base and gain their loyalty. Many of the projects we sold became long-time annuities – major companies such as Kodak, Xerox, and IBM established a customer base that continues to this day.

An independent manufacturer's representative is probably the riskiest business venture that anyone could choose – but risk is proportional to gain. We normally had a contract for a franchise to sell the manufacturers' products within a protected territory. Usually the contract could be terminated with 30 days notice by either party. It was the responsibility of the rep to hire and train the salesman, pay all operating costs of the business out of his own pocket, and to meet sales and profit goals established by the manufacturer.

A rep is a broker who does not produce the products they sell, nor do they have any control over the quality and manufacture of those products. Also, there is normally no tenure or equity with your principal. If you can make it in this kind of endeavor, you can make it in practically any business.

Being a successful manufacturer's representative requires an extremely efficient operation, top salesmen, and strong service back-up, among other things. On the other hand, once you are established, manufacturers are beating down your door wanting you to represent them. The key to success, as with most businesses, is the ability to sell and market.

Our main strategy was to cash-in on a basic weakness of the air conditioning industry, and the building industry of which it is a part. R. Buckminster Fuller, noted entrepreneur, scholar, and inventor of the geodesic dome, exposed this weakness with his observation that, "The building industry is no industry at all, but rather a collection of trades and crafts that are mired in the past. They are still in the 'place one brick upon the other and pound one nail at a time,' syndrome. Does anyone ever ask what a building weighs or how efficient it is? If the airplane industry operated in a like manner they would never have gotten off the ground."

If you operate a mercantile business there is always a threat that a competitor will open a store across the street. Walmart – the largest mercantile business in the world – got to be the largest by utilizing such a strategy. Many of their stores were built adjacent to K-Mart, and eventually they drove that mercantile giant to the edge of bankruptcy. On the other hand, our company was developed on the basis of marketing and selling unique systems and products and we had a franchise for a protected territory.

Continued success, however, depends on creating a successful end result. The most powerful sales tool is the favorable testimony of a satisfied user. In order to insure a successful end-result, we had to ensure that the systems and products sold were properly applied, properly installed, and properly serviced. This meant that the next step towards our development was to establish a service organization. If a business sells or produces a product with moving parts, it is imperative to provide in-house service, otherwise your success could be short-lived.

A businessman makes the transition from proprietor to entrepreneur when he diversifies his basic business. Abraham Lincoln told the story of a king who hired a wise man to come up with a saying that could cover all possible situations. That saying was, "This too, shall pass away." However strong your business is today, outside influences, unforeseen, can radically change your business. There are endless examples. The computer and the Internet alone have rendered thousands of businesses obsolete. Some pundits say that in the foreseeable future, writing checks, going to the post office, reading hard-copy books, magazines, or newspapers, will all be things of the past Our long-range strategy was to re-invest some of our profits in outside ventures such as real estate, and development of real estate.

Continued success also depends on maintaining a good reputation. This may sound trite because everyone thinks that they have a good reputation, but your reputation is not what you think it is – *it's what others think it is*.

Our company represented a manufacturer of rooftop air conditioning equipment and we sold a large job for the Turning Stone Casino, near Syracuse, New York. One of the units serving the main gambling hall broke down on Thanksgiving Day (the casino yields a million dollars a day profit). The problem was a faulty control device. Terry Crane, one of our key technicians, left his Thanksgiving dinner, corrected the problem, and got the casino back in operation quickly. The manufacturer did not reimburse us, nor did they even acknowledge the problem – which was radio interference with an electronic gas valve supplied with their equipment. We terminated our contract with the manufacturer to preserve our reputation, and they never sold another piece of equipment in Central New York.

Vince Lopez prophetically said, upon taking over a small, but highly profitable sales territory in Southern New York, "I have to eat from this table for the next twenty years or so, and in order to do that, I have to keep it clean."

There is an old song entitled "I Never Promised You a Rose Garden." Owning your own business is not always a rose garden, and it is definitely not for the faint of heart. There will be stress occasionally. The true course of business does not always run like a well-oiled machine. My father ran a small store, selling hardware and paints. During WWII, the business faltered because materials were hard to come by. He closed the doors and went to work for the government, being more than relieved to have someone else provide his paycheck. The saying that covers this situation is, "If you can't stand the heat, stay out of the kitchen."

A key factor that can affect successful businesses is employee greed and dishonesty. We live in an increasingly immoral world where a person's pledge does not carry the weight it once did. The green-eyed monster of greed can rear its head at any time. I hired a bright young man from a menial job with a contractor and taught him how to sell. He became very successful and was earning a six figure income, but that was not good enough, and my young protégé decided to start his own rep business. In the process he transferred orders on our books to his new company. Another key employee took kick-backs from some of our suppliers, and another, in the accounting department, just plain stole cash from the till. These experiences taught us the necessity of having some of our employees that were in sensitive positions sign contracts with non-compete clauses should they leave and start a competitive business.

While all of the above problems may cast a shadow on starting your own business, it should not deter you. The price of admission is to have your head in the game at all times. As you grow, it becomes impossible to keep your finger on all aspects, therefore, you need reliable and loyal employees to help run the ship. Our 'dream team' was a major factor toward accomplishing that goal.

CHAPTER SIX

Profile of a Salesman

All Robins are birds but all birds aren't Robins

Salesmen have a unique combination of traits and talents in their DNA not found in everyone. A person may be a 'born salesman' but it is still necessary to polish their skills to insure success. There are no accreditations, licenses, or bar exams necessary to enter this profession. A salesman could be a successful doctor, lawyer, accountant, or engineer – but the opposite is not always true. Selling is a loose profession which ranges all the way from used car salesman, to director of marketing for a major corporation. Scratch a businessman or an entrepreneur and you will usually find a salesman. It goes with the personality. A successful salesman sells products and/or services. A successful entrepreneur sells ideas, concepts, and visions. Both must be able to communicate and, in turn, motivate.

A successful salesman usually has most of the following traits:

Empathy – Webster's Dictionary defines it as "identification and understanding of the thoughts and feelings of another." To this should be added, 'The ability to sense how others react to what you say or do.' The familiar cartoon about the salesman with his foot in the door depicts a lack of empathy. Ironically, getting in the door is one of the most difficult of sales jobs. Empathy kicks in after that. Asking questions and being a good listener is an important part of empathy. I learned this lesson as a fledgling salesman peddling steam pressure-reducing valves in Upstate New York. We represented Leslie Valve Company, a small manufacturer in New Jersey. Leslie offered a rigorous five-day course to its representatives teaching about the quality, efficiency and reliability of its products. At the wrap-up each of us was presented with a demonstrator that contained a jewel-like polished brass valve nestled in a mahogany case with red velvet lining. Altogether, it was a handsome affair. I couldn't wait to hit the road and show off my newfound knowledge, and reveal the captivating demonstrator.

Locating industrial plants that might utilize steam pressure-reducing valves was called 'chasing smokestacks,' so I proceeded to drive up Route 9, along the Hudson River, looking for smokestacks. After locating one in Poughkeepsie, New York, I stopped and asked for the plant engineer. After being ushered into his office, I regaled him with the pitch (rugged construction, high quality, etc.), and showed him the demonstrator. The entire session was flawless, and I could tell he was impressed. Finally, drawing a breath, I waited for his response. He said, "Sonny – that's a mighty fine valve you got there and if we used steam in this plant that's the one we'd use." It would have saved time and embarrassment if I had the empathy to ask that simple question at the outset.

Unfortunately, empathy has become mitigated by modern communications. Bill Towne, a friend and engineering client for more than forty years, recently spoke about the loss of personal involvement in today's business world due to the advent of e-mail, faxes, cell phones, Blackberry's and iPods. He said, "I miss salesmen calling on me – especially those, like you, who tell me jokes."

Of course he was right; there is no substitute for face-to-face communication, particularly if the discussion is critical or controversial. Body language speaks volumes; a look softens or strengthens a point, a smile can disarm, and a gesture (like a picture) is worth 1000 words. I always urged our salesmen to spend a maximum amount of time in the presence of someone who could buy what they had to sell. Unfortunately, this advice is being tossed aside today in lieu of the reality of today's frenetic, computer driven, and stressful business atmosphere.

The electronic world has cut deeply into person-to-person selling. The computer, developed to reduce paperwork, has actually increased it and tied the salesman to his desk. My sons, who now run our business, can have as many as 100 e-mails during the course of a business day. The 'paperless society' vaunted by computer gurus, is a myth. Voice-mail is the antitheses of human communication. I fought the use of automated phone systems for all my years at the helm. Our 'Gal Friday' knew our customers, and they knew her. She had empathy for their needs – many times solving their problems on the spot. At the very least she could steer them in the right direction.

Automated sales presentations are another modern day marvel replacing the personal touch. Now a salesman can call on a prospect, shake hands, and plug in a VCR machine which produces a canned presentation. Is this progress? Perhaps the greatest barrier to personal communication and interaction is the ubiquitous cell phone, now enhanced by a 'Blackberry' – text messaging mobile computer. My sons and I attended a seminar recently conducted by the regional sales manager of our principal manufacturer. He was presenting a new type of air conditioning system to our engineer clients. Most of the audience was interrupted by their cell phones and text messages to the extent that they could not concentrate on the technical data being presented. Distraction, caused by cell phones and text messaging, has reached epidemic proportions, not only in automobiles, but also in conference rooms and board rooms.

Empathy is also defined by sensitivity; it is amazing how many people do not possess it. Parties or gatherings are a good place to observe the lack of sensitivity. Have you ever seen a loudmouth at a party who has backed his prey into a corner – ranting and raving with arms waving on a subject of little interest? Meanwhile, the hapless victim looks for a chance to break it off. This is an absence of empathy in action.

A sense of humor goes hand-in-hand with empathy. I have never known a great salesman who did not have a sense of humor. This is not an absolute requirement for salesmanship, but it sure helps. Humor helps to ease the tension of a sales presentation – or even a tense moment at business gatherings. Humor is like a rubber sword – it can make a point without drawing blood. A quip can disarm an argumentative person, or reveal that your prospect also has a sense of humor, which in turn can set the stage for a successful session, and sometimes a lasting relationship. Humorous and witty people have a tendency to be attracted to each other.

A good salesperson is an amateur psychologist; they can read people, find out what makes them tick, draw them out, and put them at ease. In short – they have empathy.

Persistence – Chrysler Airtemp, a competitor of Carrier Air Conditioning in the 1960s, had a distributor in Syracuse, New York (Carrier's home town) who was breaking all records selling packaged store-type air conditioners. The star salesman was not technically competent, but he out-sold all others. Chrysler's sales manager decided to visit Syracuse and make calls with this guy in order to find out how he did it.

Their first call was a bar located across the street from the Carrier plant. When the salesman walked in the door, the owner/bartender put his head in his hands and said, "Not *you* again, I've told you a dozen times we can't afford to air condition this place, and if we could, we would *have* to use Carrier." "OK," said the salesman cheerily, "I was just following up." The bulldog salesman said to his sales manager as they were leaving, "Got to follow up that guy in about a month."

More sales are lost for lack of follow-up and follow-through than for any other reason. The salesman who does not follow through is defined as a one-shot-Charlie. A story that best defines the genré – tells of a salesman who was crossing the country from New York to California introducing a new product to customers. He called his sales manager from Cleveland and said, "No sales yet, but I got a lot of 'feathers' [his definition for prospects]. Please send some expense money." Calling again from Chicago, Kansas City, and Denver, Charlie repeats the same pitch, "Lots of feathers but no sales yet." Finally, he calls from Los Angeles asking for expense money to fly home. His sales manager said in frustration, "Why don't you just glue some of those feathers on your butt and fly yourself home."

Successful people are usually good salesmen, whatever their chosen profession. Robert Congel – a leading entrepreneur and head of The

Pyramid Companies in Syracuse, sells ideas, concepts, and visions. This plaque hangs on his wall:

PRESS ON

Nothing in the world can take the place of persistence.

Talent will not: Nothing in the world is more common than unsuccessful men with talent.

Genius will not: Un-rewarded genius is almost a proverb.

Education will not: The world is full of educated derelicts.

Persistence and determination alone can secure success.

PRESS ON

Resourcefulness – One of Herb Laube's five criteria for hiring his team was, "Ability to get the job done." [The other characteristics are in Chapter Nine]. A resourceful person has a memory bank of people, places, and things that can help accomplish any project, objective, or goal that they choose.

When I was hired as Northeastern Regional Sales Manager for Remington, my job was to set up a network of manufacturer's representatives in the territory that stretched from Boston to Washington, D.C. Remington had no field sales force in this area of the country. I would hop a plane and go to these places and, after settling in a hotel room, would plan a campaign to find a rep. The main tools at my disposal were the telephone directory and the telephone. I would start by calling mechanical contractors, and after introducing myself, would ask for the names and telephone numbers of reps who sold them heating and cooling equipment – then ask who the best were.

At this juncture the most important job was to get a meeting with them (like a door-to-door salesman getting his foot in the door). If the rep was any good, the usual response was, "Sorry, but we have more equipment lines now than we can handle." The next step was to convince them to spend a few minutes in order to explore a unique business opportunity. Then, I would do some 'name dropping' by telling them of some of the top reps in the business who represented us in other areas of the country. Thus, by employing salesmanship, resourcefulness and persistence I was able to build a network of top sales representatives and went on to earn the top spot as national sales manager.

Another example of resourcefulness: Singer/Remington produced a classroom unit ventilator that had a faulty damper design that would not close in cold weather, consequently freezing heating coils. The engineering department refused to acknowledge the problem, blaming it on faulty installation, rather than admit their design error. Meanwhile, it cost the company many thousands of dollars in back-charges from customers – not to mention lost sales.

One Saturday morning, when the factory was closed, Singer/Remington's service manager (Lou Rapini) took a unit from the production line, rigged up a modified damper mechanism that he had designed, and installed it in the product lab for testing. Monday morning, he called management together and presented the modified product. After thorough testing, the engineering department reluctantly agreed that the damper worked well. The faulty units in the field were retrofitted with Lou's damper design and subsequent manufacturing production incorporated the redesigned damper mechanism. The problem was resolved.

Shortly after our company began, I hired Lou Rapini as our service manager.

Positive Mental Attitude (PMA) – Two little boys scramble down the stairs to find out what is in their Christmas stockings – stuffed and hanging on the mantle. The pessimist complains that he didn't get all he asked for. The optimist, finding horse dung in his stocking gleefully says,

"We have a pony – I just haven't found him yet." The glass is half-empty, the glass is half-full – is all about attitude. So is the solution to most of life's problems. Whether you think you can, or you think you can't – you're right!

There is an old Navy adage that tells of Admirals seated around a war table. If they want to do something, they will look in the regulations and find a clause that will allow them to do it. If they don't want to do something, they will look in the *same regulations*, and find a clause that won't allow it. The name of that tune is – attitude.

One of the greatest challenges of my life was obtaining a pilot's license, and, beyond that, becoming an instrument-rated pilot. Positive mental attitude is a prime requisite for pilots – I never met a negative wimp in the friendly skies. All of the basic requirements of salesmanship are in a pilot's psyche – resourcefulness, analytical ability, problem-solving ability, overcoming obstacles, keeping a cool head in a crisis – and tons of positive mental attitudes. Many of the reps that I worked with around the country were pilots. Can you imagine taking off into gray foreboding skies (with the proper weather briefing of course) without the attitude that you could handle whatever is out there?

One of the main instruments in the cockpit is the attitude indicator that shows the relationship of the wings to the horizon. Since you lose ground reference when you're in the clouds – this becomes the prime instrument to indicate that the wings are 'straight and level.' Should you blunder into a thunderstorm, the instructions are, "hunker down and fly attitude." If the plane gets knocked all over the sky, gets into an upset attitude, and falls into a spin – the game is usually over. So you hunker down in your seat, tighten your seat belt, concentrate on the artificial horizon, and 'fly attitude.' This is also a good procedure when the inevitable storms of life come along.

The successful salesman spends a lifetime accomplishing things that others say are impossible, overcoming obstacles that others say are insurmountable, and selling people who don't want to be sold. What drove

Columbus to venture into uncharted oceans despite the generally held theory that he would fall off the edge of the earth? What possessed Sir Edmund Hillary to climb Mt. Everest when scientists warned that man could not survive at those altitudes? The answer is *optimism, self-confidence,* and a *positive mental attitude.* This is the lever that moves the world. It is standard equipment in the salesman's kitbag.

Professionalism – The sales profession is not highly regarded because many salesmen are simply not professional. A survey in *Parade Magazine* listed the top ten professions with respect to public image. Doctors were on the top of the list and – predictably – salesmen were at the bottom. I have never seen just 'Salesman' on a calling card –Sales Manager, Sales Consultant, Sales Associate, and Sales Representative – but never just 'Salesman.'

Of course, salesmen range all the way from between-jobs to director of marketing. The successful salesperson, however, is a professional – professional in their dress, professional in the way they conduct business, and efficient in their utilization of time. The Hippocratic Oath states, 'First do no harm' – the professional salesman's oath should be, 'First, waste no time' – yours or your customer's. Perhaps no other endeavor is as closely tied to the axiom that 'time is money.'

Time is the major resource of every businessman, but it is absolutely critical for the professional salesman, because there is so little time available for actual selling. According to marketing statistics, the average salesperson spends less than 20 percent of their time doing person-to-person selling. The successful salesman must plan travel, meetings, and paperwork to maximize personal selling time. They should never call on a prospect without an appointment. The salesman who says, "I was in the area and decided to drop by" – has no respect for your time or theirs. While not wasting the time of a prospect, I was never defensive about *taking* their time. Whether or not my prospect realized it, I had important information to benefit their business.

The strongest motivation for any business person is hope of profit, or fear for loss of profit. If you can show a prospect how your product or service will benefit them – you can usually make the sale.

Character – Character comes from the Greek word 'to mark' as in 'my mark is my bond.' If the business world practiced character and honesty, most lawyers would be out of a job. Character, which is essential for success over the long haul, is difficult to define and qualify. A litmus test for any action should be, 'is it honest and is it fair?' Always do what you say you will do; 'I will get back to you' should be a commitment rather than a put-off, and 'I will take care of it' must be an ironclad contract.

We have all observed men of great talent who stumbled on the way up the ladder of success – because they became greedy, cut corners, cheated, lied, or stole. John Z. DeLorean was a bright young star at General Motors in the 1970s. At various times he headed both the Chevrolet and Pontiac Divisions, and he was being groomed for President of General Motors. DeLorean left to form his own automobile manufacturing company in the 1980s, and produced a pretty good sports car called the 'DeLorean.' It seemed inevitable that both the car and the man would be a success. However, John got greedy, misappropriated funds, got into drugs, fell into trouble with the law, lost his company, and died a broken man.

With success, some people grow – while others just swell. Greed and an over-active ego bring many down. Michael Douglas, playing the part of an inside trader in the movie "Wall Street," enthralled a meeting of stockholders when he delivered the now-famous "Greed is good" speech. Unfortunately, Wall Street today is driven by two emotions – greed (Bulls) and fear (Bears). The end result is an unstable economy. What America needs is character and honesty in the stock market – and all business dealings.

Problem-Solving Ability – Solve a problem and make a sale (as the saying goes). It never ceases to amaze me that most salesmen believe that their primary objective is to get an order. In reality, this is a byproduct of their effort. The world is full of order-takers, but the truly successful salesman views his prospect as someone with a business problem who needs help. Selling must be defined from the standpoint of benefits to your prospective customer – whether it will enhance life, make a process more efficient, reduce operating cost, or simply cost less. Define your product or service in terms of *benefits* – this is the essence of salesmanship.

The other side of the problem-solving coin is what happens after the sale when something goes wrong. Many see this as a negative – we see it as the ultimate selling situation. When a customer asks us about product guarantees we tell them (tongue-in-cheek) that the only real guarantee is that eventually, something will fail. Our salesmen are taught that their primary function is service after the sale. If the product is always shipped to the right place at the right time and never malfunctions, there is no need for a sales representative; the customer could order it from a catalogue, or the Internet.

Many manufacturers think that their only obligation is to design, manufacture and ship their products. Many begrudgingly deal with warranty problems as an item on the loss side of the ledger. They look for every loophole to avoid a claim. The successful salesman understands that his existence is justified when the product does not perform.

Enthusiasm – Enthusiasm is an infectious thing. If a person is enthusiastic about what they say and do, usually their audience is also. It is almost impossible not to be swept up in someone's enthusiasm – providing that it is sincere and not feigned. Try *not* to ignore the TV pitch man who waxes excitedly about the latest gadget.

If a salesperson is not enthusiastic about what they are selling, can their prospect be enthusiastic about buying it? If the salesperson is not enthused about what they sell, then they should be selling (or doing) something else.

Communicative Skills – Selling is all about communicating and, therefore, being a good speaker is a great asset. Unlike many of the foregoing qualities that are inborn in the sales personality, public speaking usually must be taught. The best advice we always give to anyone interested in a selling career is to take the Dale Carnegie Course. Public speaking teaches organization of ideas, thoughts, and presentation. It also teaches diction and voice projection. When a person can stand in front of a group and make a presentation, it is analogous to a batter swinging three bats before stepping up to the plate – compared to one-on-one presentations. Herb Laube was the best public speaker I ever knew. He taught that preparedness is essential for giving an effective presentation. The major points can usually be boiled down to five so that you can memorize them by ticking them off on your fingers. A more complex subject may take ten.

Laube taught that the five major factors of a good speech are:

1- An arresting opening
2- An interesting close
3- Know your subject
4- Speak distinctly
5- Practice, practice, practice

Knowing your subject beforehand is vital to success. I always write the presentation the way it will be given and then practice it out loud several times. This method enables you to be sure it flows properly, and to memorize the contents. Then put the script on the podium as a backup in case you lose the way or forget an item. Winston Churchill usually practiced his soul-stirring speeches in a bathtub (with drink in hand) reciting over and over until the material was memorized. Fear of public speaking is right up there with fear of flying for many. While a successful businessman has to overcome his fear of flying in order to travel great distances efficiently, a salesperson has to overcome their fear of public speaking in order to achieve their goals.

Charisma – This is certainly among the optional attributes and we all know 'low key' salesmen who get along. However, a person who lights up a room by walking into it, who commands attention when they speak, who draws eyes like a magnet – has one hell-of-an-advantage over someone who does not. Charisma is hard to define; most are born with it, but it never works if you try to put it on, and most who have it do not flaunt it. Good looks are not the key. Think of Winston Churchill – average looking, uninspiring of stature, yet his every word lifted a nation from the depths of despair – to victory in World War II.

The successful salesperson likes people and likes to be around them. They love life, and usually love their jobs. They are positive thinkers, good communicators, and they usually have a joke in their hip pocket. People are attracted to them and they are attracted to people. As a result, successful salespeople enjoy a higher standard of living and normally enjoy life to the fullest. America has created the best climate for selling – and we have the best sales people in the world. This great country creates demand where there is none and new markets where none existed. Whether it is automobiles or appliances, tools or toys, computers or cell phones – first ingenuity creates the product, and then salespeople create the markets.

Nothing happens until somebody sells something.

CHAPTER SEVEN

Profile of an Entrepreneur

Find a need and fill it

The classic entrepreneurial story is told of an immigrant who lands on our shores with only the clothes on his back and a few dollars in his pocket. Immediately, he goes to a newspaper stand and buys some newspapers for five cents (this is an old story) then goes to the traffic island of a busy intersection and hawks them for ten cents to motorists on their way to work. With the proceeds from the day's sale, this bright young man is able to buy twice as many papers to sell the next day. Pretty soon he buys his papers direct from the publisher and hires other people to sell them on other busy intersections. Eventually this industrious, innovative, budding entrepreneur – without the benefit of education and barely able to speak the language – starts his own media distribution business, and another self-made millionaire joins the ranks.

Find a need and fill it; whether it is a widget, a service, or an idea – this is the basis of entrepreneurship. As with salesmanship, much of the ability to see a business opportunity is born within the entrepreneur, who has the inbred talent to turn wishes and dreams into reality. Einstein opined that "Genius is one percent inspiration and 99 percent perspiration." Likewise, creating a business, particularly if there is no precedent for its need, requires dedication, discipline, and downright hard work. Ideas are a dime a dozen. We all daydream 'what if' – but few are able to say 'I can' – and even fewer are able to reflect that – 'I did.'

Having a life-long passion for automobiles triggered my first entrepreneurial adventure. Our high school was near an automobile showroom, and many of my lunch hours were spent sitting in cars day-dreaming of the day I would be able to drive my own car. When that day came, my family couldn't afford to buy one for me, but my credo has always been "Where there's a will, there's a way." So I started looking for a way.

43

Helping my mother get groceries at a nearby supermarket caused me to observe that some housewives had their groceries packed in boxes and delivered to their homes. In the 1950s it was rare to have more than one car per household, and it was usually necessary for the breadwinner to use that car to commute to work – long before there were two breadwinners in the family.

A week's groceries were too heavy for a woman to carry home and that was why the store had a delivery service. I was told by a clerk that an independent service picked up the groceries and delivered them for 45 cents per box. Further inquiry revealed that their delivery man was quitting. I asked for, and got, the job – arranging to do the deliveries after school and weekends. Fortunately, we found a used 1935 Ford delivery van for $35 dollars.

Unwittingly, I had become an entrepreneur at the tender age of sixteen. There was one more hurdle to overcome, however, before being able to drive the van. It was classified as a commercial vehicle and required a commercial driver's license – a person had to be eighteen to get a commercial drivers license and I was two years short of the legal age. Where there's a will, there's a way – painting a moustache on my face with mascara in order to appear a little older, I went to the license bureau and got the commercial license. The clerk never did the math while looking at my birth certificate.

The income from this first business venture grew to $70 a week, which was more than many people made at their full-time jobs in the 1950s. However, the entrepreneurial spirit had to go on the back burner after graduating from school. College was out of question, financially, therefore the main thrust was simply to make a living.

The entrepreneurial drive reappeared 18 years later when the frustration of working for a large corporation became unbearable.

The business was successful from the beginning, but we soon learned that being an independent manufacturer's representative was one of the most insecure enterprises of all. In order to understand this, it is necessary to understand that most manufacturers cannot afford to create a nationwide network of sales offices, and even if they could, finding and training such a sales force is an overwhelming undertaking. Consequently, manufacturers usually contract with independent sales representatives in each of the one-hundred major marketing areas of the country.

Usually this contract, which is one-sided in favor of the manufacturer, is a franchise for a given territory. It states that the representative must provide and staff local sales facilities. In many cases, if the manufactured product contains moving parts, the contract may include the requirement for local service facilities – very much like an automobile dealership. Furthermore, the contract usually states that all sales and service personnel must be factory trained. In turn, the manufacturer pays a commission on goods sold. Often the contract establishes yearly sales quotas and usually contains a provision that states "Either party may cancel with 30 days advance notice."

The rep must make a sizeable investment with virtually no guarantee of tenure. This means very little equity, other than customer relationships – which are not resalable on the open market. The landscape is littered with reps that have been fired and replaced with direct factory sales offices – sometimes because they are too successful. Often, after the rep has established a business base, the manufacturer determines that he can hire direct factory salesmen for less than the commission paid to an independent sales force.

A fellow sales rep, who sold office supplies, rented space in our office building. He invented (but unfortunately did not patent) "White-Out" – the little bottles of white liquid that secretaries used to correct mistakes on paper. Dan Brisk and his wife produced the product by filling the little bottles by hand on a picnic table in their garage. They then sold the product to their local customers, and also sold it to the national office-supply distributor that they represented. White-Out was so successful that our friend Dan could not keep up with the demand, so the distributor produced the product himself, and in the process terminated Dan as their representative. In the words of Al Pacino's drug dealing boss in the movie Scarface – "Never underestimate the other guy's greed."

A favorite story comes from "Tales of Arabian Nights." It tells of a concubine from a Harem that tells her Sheik a story every night with a conclusion the following night. Thus, she stays alive another day because of the Sheik's curiosity. She lives from day-to-day because of her wit and cunning.

That's pretty much the way independent manufacturer's representatives survive. Achieving anything resembling security requires establishing business interests independent of the manufacturer's franchise. Our first move was to create a separate company around our service department. PASCO was started by spiriting away Singer/Remington's national service manager. Lou Rapini was one of the first of our 'Dream Team' that we hired.

The next business venture created the third leg on our stool of diversity. My partner, Ron Munn, and I bought the office building we rented space in. At this juncture we created a separate partnership completely independent from our sales and service companies. M&M Development, our real estate company, provided depreciation tax advantages and bolstered our personal net worth.

It is not how much money you make that determines your wealth, but rather how much you can keep. Dipping our toes into the real estate business opened another world of investment, carrying with it additional diversity and security. Few people understand that developers seldom risk much of their own money – if they work it right. With a strong personal financial statement, a little imagination, and some common sense, almost anyone can achieve success in this fascinating field of endeavor.

Our next move was to buy a run-down local apartment house at a bargain price from an owner who was in financial difficulty. Owning and operating property does not require much personal involvement if you structure it correctly. We hired a contractor to spiff up the apartments (a little paint and some new appliances did the trick). Next, we found a real estate agent to manage rentals and take care of the property. Soon the place was humming. Establishing positive cash flow from the beginning gave us income and set the stage for turning the property a few years later for 300 percent return on our original investment. Additionally, we carried the mortgage on the resale at a healthy rate of interest.

My biggest move into the development business was a private venture independent of M & M Development. We lived on Owasco Lake – one of the Finger Lakes of Central New York. An article in the August 1985 edition of *National Geographic Magazine* featured Owasco Lake, dubbing it, "Unparalleled in all the World." There was a 50-acre site on a point at the north end of the lake, and we used to visualize having a home within that beautiful spread of meadows, trees and magnificent lakeshore.

It was owned by the Emerson Foundation (a philanthropic entity) and designated as "forever wild." The Emerson Foundation had turned it into a summer camp for the Boy Scouts of America. Our sons camped there. Teepees and Indian-style Hogans surrounded a sleepy little brook which emptied into the lake. This magnificent parcel was the most beautiful piece of land anywhere in the picturesque Finger Lakes.

In 1985 the attorney for the Emerson Foundation advised the principals that they could no longer own a non-income producing asset in a tax-free foundation. The property was then put up for sale. We put together a partnership of some of the local landed gentry, bid for the property, and acquired it. Thus, began the development of Martin Point which, beyond its beauty, was an historic landsite rich in the romance of the past. Among other factors, it was the residence of New York Governor Enos Throop, who presided during the Civil War era. General George Armstrong Custer was a frequent visitor to the Throop Mansion at Martin Point.

Beauty and history soon melded into the task of developing this environmentally sensitive land into home sites and beyond that – turning a profit. We learned many valuable lessons. First of all, whenever someone tries to accomplish a waterside development project such as this, the local governments and environmentalists will immediately line up against the developer (a cartoon appeared in the local newspaper showing deer being driven from their habitat by the greedy developers who would rape the landscape to line their pockets). After endless presentations, injunctions, and fighting those who simply are opposed to change, construction started.

It took another ten years to build out. Was it worth it? Well – when you factor in the education, the pleasure of accomplishment, and the joy of living in this breath-taking environment (each of the partners got prime lakefront lots) – the answer is yes. However, development on this scale is not for the faint-of-heart.

Auburn, New York has a rich legacy of entrepreneurs and industrialists. At the turn of the 20th century it was one of the major manufacturing hubs in America. International Harvester was the world's largest manufacturer of farm machinery – its expansive facilities stretched over 20 acres within the growing city. A spin-off, Columbian Rope Company, would go on to become one of the nation's largest suppliers of rope. American Locomotive invented and produced the first diesel/electric locomotive engines and was the world's leader in stationary steam engines.

Dunn & McCarthy, one of this country's leading producers of quality shoes, featured its Enna Jettick brand – the Gucci shoe of its day. Auburn also became a manufacturing center for carpets led by Firth Carpet Company, and General Electric employed more than 1,500 people to build semi-conductors at its expansive facility.

Remington Air conditioning Division, which started operation in 1950, and was succeeded by McQuay, is the only major industry left in Auburn today.

Why did Auburn deteriorate from a boom town in the 1920s to its current level with abandoned factory buildings everywhere, and empty stores and offices downtown? The answer is the rust belt syndrome that affects almost every city in Upstate New York. In many cases, the businesses and industries that supported those communities no longer exist and high taxes, high utility costs, union problems and uncompetitive labor rates are driving the remaining firms to relocate to Southern States or offshore.

Fortunately, Auburn is blessed with a cadre of successful businessmen, industrialists, and an unusual breed of entrepreneurial philanthropists who have become dedicated to the task of rebuilding the city to its former standing as one of the finest communities in which to live and work.

John Bisognano, was a poor immigrant who settled in Auburn at the turn of the 20th century. In order to scratch out a living, he acquired a horse and wagon – delivering fruits and vegetables house-to-house during the day, and coal – which he scraped off the ground from railroad-car spills – by night.

John Bisgrove (he changed his surname because no one could pronounce Bisognano) went on to build Red Star Trucking Company, which would become the largest regional trucking company in America. When John retired, his sons Jack and Jerry took over the operation. Consequently they sold the business in 1984. At that juncture, both brothers decided to devote the rest of their lives to investing the fortunes they derived from the sale of Red Star to helping people in need – and aiding the communities that fostered their personal wealth.

Jack and Jerry Bisgrove founded the Stardust Foundation of Central New York in 2007 – the name derived from the financial dust that emanated from the sale of Red Star. They pledged $15 million to support community organizations for health care, education, youth care, arts, art, and many other functions in the quest to improve the quality of life in Auburn and Cayuga County. I am proud to be a part of this great organization.

The Stardust Foundation has also partnered with other philanthropic organizations including the Emerson Foundation and the Allyn

Foundation. A significant portion of their investment was the refurbishing and rebuilding of the downtown area in order to provide facilities that will attract business, commerce, and industry to Cayuga County. This venture has literally changed the face of downtown Auburn. The first major project was "Auburn's Creative Corridor" – that was a renovation of abandoned buildings and eyesores into a charming block of shops and offices with architecture that melds the Auburn of yesteryear with the functionality of today. The centerpiece of the corridor includes the "Stardust Entrepreneurial Institute" – an incubator for new businesses, and Auburn Musical Theatre – which will combine with the Merry-Go-Round Theatre at Emerson Park in order to bring theatre to downtown once again.

Michael J. Falcone, fellow Auburnian and founder of the Pioneer Companies, is also part of the quest to rebuild downtown Auburn. Beyond owning some of the buildings that constitute the Creative Corridor, Falcone is building a 91-room Hilton Gardens Inn and Conference Center which will anchor the entire project.

Research conducted by the Stardust Foundation indicated that there is a need for an upscale hotel and conference center in the heart of the Finger Lakes. Shermans Travel LLC – a widely respected New York City review and rating agency – rates the Finger Lakes Region as "The Number One Lakeside Retreat in the World." Falcone has put together a partnership of local business leaders to build this new hotel center and, once again, Modular Comfort Systems is pleased to be a partner for the creation of this ambitious project.

Thus, a group of people, born and brought up in Auburn, have invested their time, talents, and millions of dollars for a dream – that Auburn will be a hub of business and industry once again so that our children's children will not have to leave this little piece of paradise in order to seek their fortunes.

Over the past 50 years I have had the pleasure of working with many of the top entrepreneurs in the country. There are common threads that run through all:

Ideas, Ideas, Ideas – Everything starts with an idea. Nothing is as powerful as an idea whose time has come. Idea men – the people who invent products, processes, machinery, stores, and services – are the core of this country's greatness. America gives anyone the freedom to pursue their dreams. The entrepreneur always has his ear to the ground, eyes open, and is always thinking of a better or more efficient way of doing things.

Timing – Seldom is success the result of being at the right place at the right time. This is a placebo for the ne'er-do-wells, who envy the success of others. Mostly, entrepreneurs make their own timing, because they are always thinking ahead of the crowd. The current buzz-phrase for this phenomenon is, "thinking outside the box." This type of person does not waste time predicting the future – they make the future. However, it is wise to heed the words of my mentor Herb Laube who said, "It is good to lead the parade but don't get so far ahead that you can't hear the tune the band is playing."

Vision – Robert Congel, a developer in Syracuse, New York, cashed in on the trend of moving downtown stores to the burgeoning suburbs in the 1970s. His vision created many suburban shopping malls and he became one of the most successful mall developers in the country. His greatest challenge was the development of the Carousel Mall, on the shores of Onondaga Lake in Syracuse.

The site he chose was probably the greatest example of an industrial rape of a beautiful environment. The lake itself had become the most polluted body of water in the country. Solvay Process, a producer of soda ash (Arm & Hammer Baking Soda) built its soda ash distillation plant adjacent to the lake and pumped its limestone waste – a byproduct of soda ash – into giant waste beds on the edge of the lake. The waste beds were designed to leach the milky waste into the lake. This created a toxic sludge that killed all the wildlife and created an odor for miles around. To add to this sorry situation, Syracuse pumped its sewage to a plant on the shore of the lake, and also bled sewage into the lake. As if all this was not enough, a giant metal junkyard had existed on the site of the mall producing corrosive and toxic material that seeped into the soil. Oh! And adjacent to the site was 'Oil City' – a large complex of gas tanks that seeped petroleum into the surrounding soil.

When news of development of the Carousel Mall was made public, everyone thought Congel was out of his mind – but this entrepreneur could see beyond the pollution and the stench to a beautiful shopping mall which overlooked a beautiful lake. It took years to clean up the lake – an effort that continues to this day – stop the sewage leak, dredge the building site of toxic material, and remove the oil tanks. Today, the Carousel Mall sets on the shore of a recovering Onondaga Lake, instead of a stinking polluted toxic waste site and a rusting batch of oil tanks. This environmental miracle exists because of the vision of a man.

Persistence – Success in any field of endeavor requires persistence. The field is littered with those who started with a bang and petered out in the stretch. Abraham Lincoln failed in his run for political office several times before winning the presidency. If at first you don't succeed try, try again. This should be the theme song for the budding entrepreneur.

Henry Ford labored long and hard after hours in a little shed behind his small house in Dearborn, Michigan, in order to build his first 'Horseless Carriage.' When it was complete, he discovered that he couldn't get it through the door so he knocked a hole in the wall. His first automobile manufacturing venture was a failure. Ford then got new backing and started again. The Ford Motor Company did not take off until Henry had an epiphany.

Realizing that the first automobiles were toys for the wealthy, Ford finally understood that in order to sell his cars in volume, they would have to be cheap enough so that the average worker could afford to buy them. He then designed the famous "Model T" that was rugged, reliable, and affordable, selling for $250 dollars. Then he designed the moving production line, and in an unprecedented move for the early 1900s, increased the salary of his workers to five dollars a day thereby insuring that his own workers could buy the automobiles they produced. The rest is history.

Pyramiding success – When Robert Congel started his development empire, he created "The Pyramid Companies" which was more than a name. Congel had a brilliant idea to pyramid his success by creating satellite businesses that would be involved in the construction of his malls and other buildings. His approach was to find accomplished people in the fields of general construction, air conditioning, plumbing, and electrical contracting – as well as various other related fields such as real estate and management. He then put them in business and owned 50 percent of their companies. Later when they became established, Congel allowed them to buy out his interest.

One of these bright young men had been a sales engineer from Carrier – his name was Ron Woodcock. When I first met Ron, his small business was housed in a trailer in the parking lot behind Congel's office building. I was impressed. He was a young guy, like me, who was frustrated by working for a big corporation. Subsequently, Ron packed it in and started his own mechanical contracting business with Congel's help. I sold Ron on the concept of using water source heat pump systems in Pyramid buildings. We did our first major project, Widewaters Office Park in DeWitt, New York, which was a huge success. Ron and I went on to do millions of square feet of Pyramid buildings, and many more developer buildings in Upstate New York.

One of Congel's partners for the many shopping malls built throughout the Northeast was Michael J. Falcone. After the development of Widewaters, Falcone branched out from Pyramid in order to concentrate on office buildings. He envisioned an ongoing need for modern, efficient office buildings in downtown Syracuse and other upstate cities. Falcone founded 'The Pioneer Companies' much along the lines of The Pyramid Companies, but with emphasis on modern technology which would enhance the comfort of the occupant while lowering owning and operating costs.

One Park Place, in the heart of downtown Syracuse, was a breakthrough in efficient air conditioning systems, combining Total Electric Decentralized Water Source Heat Pump Systems, and Direct Digital Computerized (DDC) energy management systems. My company, Modular Comfort Systems, partnered with Pioneer to accomplish a breakthrough in energy efficiency. One Park Place consumed less than half of the energy consumption for heat, light and power – compared to all other conventional office buildings locally. The building also utilized renewable energy. It stands to this day as a model for 'green' building technology.

Business acumen – An idea or a vision cannot go far without implementation, and that requires developing a business, or at least allying with a business, that can carry your product and/or service into the marketplace. Many inventors and entrepreneurs fall short in this area.

A doctor friend of mine in Auburn had invested $100,000 in order to bankroll a brilliant young electronics engineer and start an electronics control business. My partner and I were called upon to be on his board of directors because our company sold and installed electronic controls. We examined the products that AT Controls had developed and were impressed.

When we asked about plans to market the products, the brilliant young engineer was quite abrupt, and advised us that he was far too busy developing products to be concerned with sales. He continued to develop product and pretty soon the company went through the seed money. Our doctor friend managed to sell another $100,000 of stock to his friends and fellow doctors. One day I invited my friend to lunch and tried, as diplomatically as possible, to tell him that if he didn't get the engineer out of the lab and on the street to sell product, or hire a salesman, the company wouldn't make it. Unfortunately, by the time he got around to understanding the problem it was already too late and AT Controls had to close its doors.

Another example of the need for business acumen was Willis Carrier, who founded the air conditioning industry. Carrier Engineering began operation in 1908, and foundered in the 1930s because Willis Carrier, who was a genius by any measure, could not cope with the expanding demand for the products he developed. Growth required financing, recruiting sales talent, marketing, and manufacturing. However, Willis Carrier was not effective in this arena. He preferred to operate in his research laboratory.

Enter El Ray Cloud Wampler, a banker from Chicago, who was a major stockholder and board member. Wampler was asked by the board of directors to take over the operations of the company, in order to avoid almost certain bankruptcy. Willis Carrier was very happy to retreat to his beloved laboratory and let Cloud Wampler build Carrier into "The World's Number One Air Conditioning Manufacturer."

In the final analysis, the entrepreneurial adventure seldom begins with eureka! Many entrepreneurial successes come with modifying the ideas, or the work of others. It may only come after years of research and trial and error requiring a slow process of improving upon tried and true ideas, often, a percolation of the work and experiences of others. Herb Laube called it "design by analogy." The greatest example of this was a computer geek by the name of Bill Gates.

The fabric of a successful entrepreneur is woven within the qualities of a successful salesman, and a successful businessman. They all start with establishing goals early in life. Sad to say, but the average person has no goals in life other than to make a living – and that is why they are average (see Epilogue 2). They settle for whatever comes along. On the other hand, the latent entrepreneur has visions – visions of a better life – visions of a better world. They see things not as they are, but as they could be, and of course they have imagination and the ability to visualize what others cannot see. The entrepreneur is never happy with the status quo and they usually have abundant energy which drives them to excel at whatever endeavor they choose. Their spirit, foresight and visions are intertwined with the development of mankind. Chances are we would still be swinging from trees had not the first entrepreneur captured fire and brought it into the cave.

CHAPTER EIGHT

The Art of Leadership

"The buck stops here"

The opening days of World War II were frightening for America as well as the rest of the free world. As a child of eight, I huddled around our Motorola mahogany console radio every night with my parents and sisters listening to the war news. Hitler had swept through Western Europe behind the dreaded Blitzkrieg (lightning attack), and stood at the shore of the English Channel. From there he could see England, and his last conquest for the domination of Europe – and the world. The Japanese had virtually destroyed America's naval force in the Pacific and stood poised to attack us on our western coast. Defense wardens on both coasts patrolled the beaches and America turned out its lights at night. We heard the wail of air raid sirens for the first time in our history.

Only two leaders of men and country stood between the world and the incredibly evil regimes of Germany and Japan.

Winston Churchill, a man of modest physical stature, showed little emotion for people places or things and lived for politics. He was made prime minister as the war broke out, following a cowardly Neville Chamberlain who practically handed Hitler the continent of Europe on a silver platter – following the infamous treaty signed in Munich. Chamberlain called it, "Peace in our time." Churchill replied; "An appeaser is someone who feeds a crocodile hoping it will eat him last."

From that time on Churchill's passion and obsession – indeed his only persistent thoughts and ideas were to defeat Germany. He was a brilliant orator and writer – as are most leaders – and as it turned out, the pen was mightier than the sword.

Churchill addressed the House of Commons on June 18, 1940 in his deep monotone voice saying:

"Hitler knows that he will have to break us in this island or lose the war. If we can stand up to him, all Europe may be free and the life of the world may move forward into broad, sunlit uplands. But if we fail, the whole world, including the United States, including all we have known and cared for, will sink into the abyss of a new Dark Age made more sinister and perhaps more protracted by the lights of perverted science. Let us therefore brace ourselves to our duties, and so bear ourselves that, if the British Empire and its Commonwealth lasts for a thousand years, men will say, 'This was their finest hour!'"

For seventy-six nights of that fateful summer of 1940 Germany filled the sky with bombers and reduced London to rubble. Most mornings Churchill was there to help set up food, shelter, and medical care for the survivors. During that time, he also addressed a group of Naval Officers with perhaps the greatest of his inspirational oratory; his entire speech was, "Never give in. Never, never, never, never give in."

Franklin Delano Roosevelt became President of the United States in 1932, during one of the worst periods of this country's history. He had been stricken with poliomyelitis in 1921 and remained a cripple for the rest of his life, but the public never knew it. We respected our leaders then much more than today, and the press avoided taking pictures of him in a wheel chair. Roosevelt's socialistic policies are still argued – such as withholding taxes from paychecks which gave government great control over the population and thrust big government upon us; however, his masterful leadership and dedication to the principles that America holds dear was never in doubt.

Just as this country was emerging from a long and arduous depression, the winds of war were brewing in Europe. America was still an isolationist nation but when Japan attacked Pearl Harbor on December 7, 1941 ("A day that will live in infamy" – FDR), there was no decision to be made. As

Churchill led his country, so Roosevelt led America with his weekly 'Fireside Chats' declaring "We have nothing to fear but fear itself."

Just as Britain had its finest hour, the United States fulfilled the prophecy of Japanese Admiral Isoroku Yamamoto after he led the attack on Pearl Harbor. Yamamoto poignantly remarked, "I fear all we have done is awakened a sleeping giant and filled him with a terrible resolve."

Sometimes leadership comes from strange forces. Movie actor Ronald Reagan was elected president in 1981 during one of our most troubled post-war periods. The U.S. economy had been in decline for sixteen years as a result of tax increases, dollar devaluations, wage and price controls, minimum wage hikes, misguided spending, pandering to unions, protectionist measures, and a litany of misguided governing. The crisis had reached critical mass with President Jimmy Carter's "malaise" (as this book goes to press our country faces identical problems under the equally inept leadership of President Barak Obama).

Enter Ronald Reagan stage right with his handsome demeanor, entrancing rhetoric, and razor sharp wit ("Don't worry about the deficit – it's too big to fail"). The liberal press derided this movie actor and his "trickle-down economics." Also, we were in a death grip struggle with the Soviet Union in a war that was 'cold' in name only.

Reagan enacted his first major piece of legislation in August of 1981 and it included sweeping tax cuts reducing the maximum rate from 70 percent to 50 percent – and the lowest rate from 14 percent to 11 percent. Reaganomics moved America towards lower, flatter tax rates, sound money, freer trade and less regulation, all of which changed people's behavior with respect to working, investing, and producing. Reagan's first year at the helm also included a strike by the federal air traffic controllers. His response to this illegal action was to fire the lot of them, and replace them with military personnel until permanent replacements could be found and trained. It was a brave and dramatic act, given the degree of union control in our country at the time, but his action sent a message that it was not business as usual. Consequently, this action took our country out of the grip of self-serving union officials for many years to come (today we are once again back in the grip of self-serving union officials).

Reagan also fired a shot across the bow of Soviet leadership by declaring that "The only morality that they recognize is what will further their cause meaning they reserve unto themselves the right to commit any crime, to lie, to cheat, and this is something the United States needs to keep in mind when dealing with Moscow." The media responded with a collective gasp and he was widely criticized – but this set the tone of our future relations with Russia, and led to Reagan's famous speech at the Brandenburg Gate in June 1987: "Mr. Gorbachev – tear down this wall." Not only did this dynamic address lead to the reunification of Germany – but eventually the collapse of the Soviet Union also.

In July 2011, Eastern Europe and London celebrated eight days of Ronald Reagan on the occasion of his centenary year. Celebrations took place in Krakow, Budapest, Prague, and London. At the unveiling of Reagan's statue in Budapest's Freedom Square, Prime Minister Viktor Orban said: "Reagan managed change wisely and preserved peace. This is why he deserves to have a statue in Budapest. In tearing down the distorted and sick ideologies of the 20th century, Reagan remade the world for us." At the conclusion of Orban's speech, he echoed the sentiments heard from Americans of every persuasion, "We need a Ronald Reagan today. Is he there somewhere, already? The world misses him as much as we do. It misses grand leadership as much as we do."

As said before, I learned the lessons of leadership under the tutelage of Herbert Laube – the greatest business leader I have ever encountered with a brilliant mind and the ability for concise reasoning and analysis combined with practicality (my wife Janet says that common sense is not so common) and something else he continually practiced and taught to me – intellectual curiosity.

Here is a compilation of the principles that still drive my actions and philosophies on how to run a business:

When You're in Command – Command

President Harry S. Truman was thrust into the presidency on April 12, 1945, upon the death of President Franklin Delano Roosevelt, who never confided in him about the development of the atomic bomb or the pending conflict with the Soviet Union. Truman promptly placed a plaque upon his desk which stated, "The Buck Stops Here."

He was soon to find out what a commitment that was, when as commander in chief he alone had to issue approval for dropping the atomic bomb (an act that is debated to this day). He had another tough decision to make when North Korea invaded South Korea (likewise his decision was debatable but it likely saved the entire Pacific Rim from falling into communist hands). Truman turned out to be one of America's great leaders during the tumultuous mid-20th century period.

Leadership carries with it a heavy mantle. The day people stop bringing you problems is the day you have stopped leading them. They have either lost confidence that you will help them or they have concluded that you do not care – in either case, it's a failure of leadership. Unfortunately, most CEOs in today's corporate world would fail this litmus test, as management by committee and consensus is the rule rather than the exception. I experienced this when Singer took over the operation of Remington. They instituted endless meetings, reports and procrastination, and this was a major factor for starting my own business.

Decisiveness

If you try to please everyone under your command, you will end up pleasing no-one, and lose the respect of all. I wouldn't give a hoot for a CEO who manages by consensus; you will end up avoiding the tough decisions and confronting the people who need confronting. Most importantly, you'll shrink back from firing people who need firing.

Ironically, by avoiding the difficult choices, by trying not to anger anyone, and by treating everyone equally, regardless of their contributions, the only thing that you will accomplish is to frustrate the most productive and most creative people within your group. An old bromide states that 'I am not always right but I'm always the boss' – is meant to deride leadership. To me it is a badge of courage. Herb Laube was not always right, but he was always fair and would listen to dissenting opinions – which leads me to the following axiom …

Avoid Yes-Men

You can always identify the ass-kissers among your people. They will always agree with whatever you say or do. Barry Rand, one of Xerox's legendary leaders taught his people that "if you have a yes-man working for you – one of you is redundant."

Shortly after we took on the franchise to represent Remington Air Conditioning Division, my boss Hal Walsh and I were called on the carpet by Herb Laube. We had inherited one of Remington's first installations, which was the Statler School of Hotel Administration at Cornell University (an actual hotel built on campus for training of hotel managers and accommodating and visiting parents). The factory had sold the incremental thru-wall air conditioners direct before we became their reps.

Operational problems had developed with what was a pilot installation of a new model of equipment. Herb criticized us for not properly servicing the equipment but we were not even aware of the problems. I unloaded on Laube saying, "Herb – you are wrong, and furthermore I do not work *for* you, I work *with* you – and I wouldn't work *for* you for all the money there is." Six months later Laube offered me the job of regional sales manager. It turned out that he respected those that would stand up to him when he was wrong.

Organization Charts Accomplish Nothing

Organization charts are the crutch of management, as are long-range planning and theories of management. The advent of the computer and merger-mania has loaded many trash cans with these feel-good exercises. I could never have projected the path of our business from the beginning, and I could not project it at the turn of the 21st century when it was turned over to my sons (they have more than doubled the business since then). The only thing that matters is the people you select to build and run your business on a day-to-day basis – which leads to the next axiom ...

The Art of Choosing People

As previously stated in Chapter Five – the three most useless tools for hiring are résumés, references, and an interview. Herb Laube's five criteria for hiring his key people were:

- Character
- Ability to get along
- Ability to get things done
- Capacity for judgment
- Technical competence

Actually, I have learned that you must go beyond these simple guidelines – you must ferret out attributes such as intelligence, a capacity to anticipate problems as well as solve them, loyalty, integrity, high energy drive, and a balanced ego (as I have told my sons, ego is like fire – a little fire is necessary to sustain life, but an over-active ego is like wildfire – it destroys life). How do you obtain this input in a single interview? The answer is that you cannot. It took me many years – and a few mistakes – to develop the technique.

Our business was mature by 1998 but we needed an experienced sales engineer to cover our expanding sales volume, and my retirement was looming. I had been looking for almost two years and had exhausted all hope of finding the right person locally. Through the grapevine we heard about Drew Reagan – an experienced Carrier sales engineer who was working in the company's Seattle office. He wanted to get back to Central New York in order to be closer to his family. We had a 20-minute telephone conversation and it appeared that he had the necessary talent and shared our values.

We invested in an airplane ticket and flew him in for a more in-depth conversation – and to meet my son Chris who would be taking over the sales end of the business soon. We talked for nearly three hours over dinner. There is something relaxing about dinner and a libation that puts the prospect at ease, as compared to the cold surroundings of a conference room. It was obvious after this session that Drew would fit into our operation like a glove. Subsequently, Drew has proven to be one of our top salesmen and a partner in our rapidly expanding business. Another indicator of leadership is to develop your people to be leaders for an orderly transition should something befall the head of the company. More than one business has collapsed when its leader was stricken.

The KISS Principle (Keep It Simple Stupid)

While this over-used phrase might be a little trite – nothing else describes the trend to over-complicate, which smothers the business world today. Part of the problem lies within the electronic age and TMI (Too Much Information) which overloads our brain with too many choices. However, the main problem lies with our teaching institutions that do not teach the leaders of today and tomorrow to be concise.

Herb Laube once sent me a three-page memo with a scribbled note which read, "I apologize for the length of this memo. If I had more time I could have made it shorter." He also taught that any plan, or program, or idea, or communiqué, or presentation, should be broken into no more than five parts – why? Because you can analyze or learn them by ticking them off on your fingers. Extremely complex situations might require ten parts (ten fingers).

Our government attempted to draft a health-care reform program in 2010. They drafted a document of more than 2,000 pages and sent it to the president and members of Congress to vote on. How utterly stupid was that? Had I been the leader of that bureaucratic group – I would have returned it to the sender and requested that the document be condensed to no more than 100 pages outlining the critical data needed to render a decision. No mind can decipher a 2000 page document written in legalize.

Lawyers perpetuate themselves by purposely overcomplicating things in a language that only another lawyer can decipher. There is a story told of a lawyer who moved into a small town and hung out his shingle. He was never able to get any local clients until a second lawyer moved into town and hung out his shingle.

Great leaders are great simplifiers who can cut through arguments, debates, and doubts, in order to offer solutions that everybody can understand.

Perpetual Optimism and Enthusiasm

Leo D. was an electrical engineer whose drafting board was next to mine at Sergeant, Webster, Crenshaw & Folley, the Syracuse architectural firm I worked for during the early years of my career. He continually complained about our working conditions – we should be making more money, we should have shorter hours, more vacation time, we should form a union, etc. I often thought to myself, "Leo – if you spent more time doing your job, as the rest of us do, you would be much better off." Eventually, Leo got a job with the government – which is where he belonged.

Leaders, who are negative and continually complain, engender the same behavior among the people in their charge. If they are cynical and pessimistic – likely their people will also be. That is why I believe that unionism, for the most part, has a negative influence on America. The days of the sweat shops are long gone, but the job of a union leader is still to convince his constituents that they have poor working conditions and need higher wages – otherwise they would not remain union leaders for long. Likewise our career politicians in Congress must continually give our tax dollars away to their constituents in order to stay in office. This scenario has reached critical mass, and unless our leaders face up to the situation, the future of our country looks dim.

On the other hand, the ripple effect of enthusiasm and optimism can be remarkable. The person in charge should be a cheerleader as well as organizational leader. They should not only set individual performance goals, but also continually review and encourage and convince that these goals can be achieved.

Optimism is also something that rubs off on others. If you are optimistic about the future, optimistic about your company's potential success, optimistic about achieving its goals, and optimistic about your ability to help others achieve their goals – well, that's what leadership is all about. This world is divided into two classifications – winners and losers, and I never met a winner who was not an optimist.

Be a Mentor

The Chinese believe that if you save a person's life – you are responsible for them for the rest of their life. I believe that leaders are responsible for guiding everyone under their immediate command to achieve their full potential. After being hired by Remington as regional sales manager, Herb Laube set up his key people for a management seminar. This included 'personal evaluation' – which was the fad of corporations in the 1960s. Today, this kind of intrusive evaluation is considered an invasion of privacy.

Part of the session included IQ testing. I was rated in the upper 20th percentile (which was average for our group). The instructor told me that I had sufficient intelligence to achieve anything I set my mind to. This meant that I had the brainpower to do the job and at least one of the five criteria (technical competence). Herb took it upon himself to augment the other four criteria (character, ability to get along, ability to get things done, and capacity for judgment) – by constant mentoring. We often traveled together and he would regale me with his experiences to illustrate the aforementioned attributes. What he taught could never be learned from text books. Herb invested his most valuable asset – which was his time and interest – in my development. This is the essence of mentoring.

And finally …

Lead with a Light Hand

Don't take yourself too seriously. The great leaders, from Winston Churchill, to FDR, to Ronald Reagan – all had a fine-tuned sense of humor. They could laugh at themselves as well as the foibles of others.

Don't be buffaloed by the elites and the experts. Experts often possess more raw data than judgment. Have fun in your command. Don't always run at a break-neck pace. Take the afternoon off when you've earned it. Surround yourself with people who take their work seriously – but not themselves. Spend time with your family. You are not a complete person unless your family is a success. Avoid the workaholic (they seethe with insecurity). Seek people who have balance in their lives – those who are fun to hang out with, and love to laugh; those who have non-job priorities that they approach with the same passion that they do their work. In short they have a balanced life.

I have always believed that – when you work – *work*. When you play – *play*, but don't combine the two. My sons have balanced lives and have expanded our business far beyond my expectations. They have assembled a team of sharp, dedicated 'young lions' who have swept the competition under the rug. They usually take-off at 3 p.m. on Friday afternoons to play basketball with their cohorts.

CHAPTER NINE

Marketing Myopia

The only constant is change

A Harvard University Business School professor wrote an article many years ago entitled "Marketing Myopia" in which he explains the tunnel vision that affects many companies as they grow, as markets change, and as times change.

A prime example of his treatise is our railroads. At the turn of the 20th century, railroads completely dominated the transportation and freight businesses. When the automotive industry emerged, and spawned trucks to haul freight long distances, railroad companies could have developed trucking companies – but they didn't. When airplanes started carrying passengers from coast-to-coast, the railroad giants could have developed airline companies – but they didn't.

Even though the railroad industry had the capital, the routes, and the customers to expand into these other venues, they only envisioned themselves as being in the *railroad* business, rather than the *transportation* business. Today, the railroads struggle to stay alive because airlines dominate long-distance passenger travel and trucks dominate the freight business. Ironically, today freight trains carry truck trailers on flatbeds for long-distance freight.

Detroit ruled the automotive universe from the turn of the 20th century until after WW II. Soldiers who had served in the European theatre were exposed to sports cars and other small, efficient, fun-to-drive vehicles. Some brought these cars home with them. When the Volkswagen Beetle started showing up on our shores, Detroit laughed. The reaction of the 'Big Three' was that "small cars mean small profits" and since they could sell all the automobiles they could make – why bother?

The American auto industry continued to scoff at the imports, right through the energy crises of the mid-1970s, and today the Big Three (GM, Ford, and Chrysler) are in crisis – all victims of 'marketing myopia.'

Our business was launched because of the marketing myopia of the air conditioning industry, which failed to recognize the need for more energy efficient and lower cost air conditioning systems. While our business prospered due to the marketing myopia of the Big Three – in time we came to suffer the same symptoms. Our prime company, Modular Comfort Systems, was so named to reflect our niche market, which was decentralized, self contained, air conditioning modules. We created this market that did not exist before our sales and promotional efforts. The strategy worked well for many years – until our principal manufacturer, Singer Climate Control Division, was sold to its president, Dick Snyder.

Snyder became a super-charged entrepreneur and proceeded to take "Snyder General" in a completely new direction. Soon after acquiring Singer's air conditioning business (by virtue of highly leveraged financing), he acquired McQuay, a sleepy family-owned manufacturer of chillers and central station air conditioning equipment.

Now, Snyder had two independent-rep sales forces – one for central systems and one for decentralized systems. Snyder gathered both groups together and announced that there would be a consolidation of sales representatives so that customers would have one telephone number to call in each territory. It became obvious to us that we had to take the McQuay line of chillers and central station equipment or risk losing it all. Consequently, with the scratch of a pen on paper, we became the super market, rather than the delicatessen, of air conditioning products for Upstate New York. At this juncture, we were forced to expand our operation and go head-to-head with the 'Big Three' of the air conditioning industry.

Our subsidiary company, Packaged Air Conditioning Service Corporation (PASCO) was so named because of our marketing myopia in the service business. We could never envision the company doing anything beyond repairing self-contained air conditioners on a bench in our small shop. However, the expansion of our sales business meant we also had to expand the service business to include chillers and other central station equipment.

Then a major business opportunity came our way due to the marketing myopia of the temperature control industry. Until the 1980s, there was a 'gentleman's agreement' between these two closely allied industries. Air conditioning manufacturers did not produce or sell temperature controls, and vice versa. Typically the air conditioning systems for large buildings were controlled by pneumatic or electromechanical temperature controls, which were provided and installed as a separate entity by temperature control manufacturers and installing contractors.

All this changed, with the advent of computers. The young entrepreneurs spawned by the computer industry learned to 'think outside the box' and soon realized that computers, connected to electronic temperature control actuators would make the ponderous pneumatic and electromechanical control systems obsolete. Additionally, the compact electronic control modules (ECMs) could be installed on the equipment at the air conditioning manufacturer's factory – further reducing time and labor cost for field installation.

We as entrepreneurs could also see this trend coming and structured PASCO to become purveyors and installers of Direct Digital Control (DDC) temperature control and energy management systems.

The evolution of the temperature control industry started in Silicon Valley, as did so many other enterprises. Clair Jenkins was an acquaintance of Bill Gates, and Gates opened his eyes to computer controlled electronic temperature control systems. As a result Jenkins founded Alerton Controls and PASCO became one of its first representatives. Effectually, Clair Jenkins became, to the automatic temperature control (ATC) industry what Herb Laube became to the heating, ventilating, and air conditioning (HVAC) industry.

We were able to obtain the technicians necessary for this new business venture from existing temperature control companies – who were downsizing due to loss of business. Today, the former 'Big Three' temperature control manufacturers (Honeywell, Johnson, and Powers) are no longer a dominate factor in the temperature control industry. Ironically, Honeywell eventually bought Alerton and PASCO is still one of their leading representatives.

Abraham Lincoln told the story of a king who hired a wise man to come up with a saying that would cover all possible situations. That saying was, "This too shall pass away." Ninety percent of all the technology developed since the beginning of time has occurred in the latter part of the 20th century, and the rate of change has accelerated exponentially since the turn of the 21st century. In these dynamic times, businesses rise and fall overnight and *tradition* is a dangerous mindset. Whatever business you choose – you must plan on business cycles, product cycles, economic cycles, and *change*.

The only thing that remains constant – is change.

Herbert Livingston Laube

CHAPTER TEN

The Legacy of Herbert Livingston Laube

Everyone knows that Henry Ford was the father of the American automobile. However, there were lesser known men like William 'Billy' Durant, the fast-living entrepreneur who started General Motors. General Motors eclipsed Ford in the 1930s. Likewise, almost everyone knows that Willis Carrier was the father of air conditioning, but few people know that El Ray Cloud Wampler, a banker from Chicago, rescued Carrier from certain bankruptcy in the 1930s and was responsible for making Carrier Corporation the success it is today.

And then there was Herbert Livingston Laube. Herb used to say, "If 50 percent of the people thought that I was an S.O.B. and the other 50 percent thought me a success – that would not be the problem. The problem is that 99 percent of the people don't know that I exist."

Not only did Herb Laube exist, but he also had a significant influence on the way buildings are air conditioned today. Beyond being one of the greatest entrepreneurs I have ever known, Laube became the conscience of the industry by introducing energy conservation air conditioning systems and laying the groundwork for what is known as 'Green' buildings today.

Herb was a minister's son and married a minister's daughter. He was not a religious man but he was a moral man – and he was German to the core. The family name was changed from Laubengeiger when they emigrated from Germany before WW II. Herb opined that "You do not breed a greyhound to burrow in holes for ferrets, neither do you breed a dachshund to chase down a rabbit by sight and speed." This ethnic analysis indicated his pride of heritage. Laube was convinced that his race constituted the world's best in intelligence, organizational skills, and industriousness.

Laube graduated from Iowa University. He kicked around the country for awhile joining the Navy and becoming a pilot. Subsequently, doctors discovered that he had an enlarged heart and he was forced to quit. Later Herb became a private pilot and, miraculously, lived through it. The enlarged heart did not bother him. He said, "It's like having a big engine in a small car." Amazingly, Herb enjoyed good health for most of his life. It was difficult keeping up with him while walking the streets of New York City when he was in his seventies and I in my forties.

Eventually, Herb worked his way to California where he took a job with a company called Parker Iron Works. The job didn't offer much of a challenge for him but he did manage to invent the 'Laube Concrete Gun.' The huge concrete viaducts in the Los Angeles Basin, that channel water from the nearby mountains, were built with the Laube Concrete Gun.

Next, Herb worked for Brunswick Kroeschell (B-K), which manufactured refrigeration machines for food markets. Carrier merged with Brunswick Kroechell in the 1930s and thus Laube's career with Carrier began. This dynamic young engineer had traveled the world for B-K, so his first assignment for Carrier was with their International Division. Again, he traveled the world with Carrier working in 66 countries. Herb spun many tales of his traveling experiences and he was a fascinating story teller.

Few have ever equaled this man's overall business talent. He was, all-at-once the engineer who conceived the products, the salesman who sold them, the marketing director who developed the market, and the advertising and promotional director who wrote the literature. Laube was the consummate businessman, leader, and teacher, and in today's specialized and compartmentalized corporate world, truly an enigma.

Herb set up production facilities and ran the plant with an iron fist. He often said that you could walk into a factory and, very quickly, analyze the quality of management. If the plant was dirty, disheveled, and disorganized, it spoke volumes about the management. There seems to be ample support for this philosophy – when Dunn & Bradstreet evaluate a business, they will report whether or not it has "A neat and orderly premises."

One of his many business axioms was, "What you don't spend – you make." Laube also said, "Too many pigs around the trough mean less for everyone to eat." Herb not only taught us the value of a dollar, he also taught the value of a *penny.* Everyone had a three-minute egg timer on their desk for timing long-distance calls. No one, including Herb, ever flew first-class or stayed in first-class hotels. Every expense report was reviewed, and if an item looked out of line, you were called upon to explain. He ran a tight ship, but this benefited all of us who went on to operate our own businesses.

This captain of industry was always respected, if not always revered. When the sun is shining and the wind is calm, the crew might nit-pick about the way the captain runs the ship, but when the storm rises and the waves break over the bow, it is good to have a strong hand at the wheel. That storm came in 1954 during a deep recession (the definition of a recession is when your neighbor loses his job – a depression is when *you* lose your job). The commercial construction business came to a virtual halt that year and Remington had hundreds of air conditioning units sitting in railroad boxcars that distributors could not take delivery of – nor pay for.

At the end of the year, Remington was $900,000 in debt (equivalent to more than $10 million today). Remington had given open credit to many of its customers. Herb had learned an indelible lesson that he passed on to all of his people, "Good judgment is the result of experience – which is the result of bad judgment."

A lesser man would have declared bankruptcy and gone across the street to start a new business, screwing the stockholders in the process, but Laube promised each of his creditors that if they would work with him, he would pay back every dollar – with interest. It took Remington ten years to accomplish the pledge, but eventually the company paid all its debts and returned to profitability. However, the stress took its toll on Laube and he sold the business to Singer Company in 1966.

Laube later admitted that he had given up the ship too soon. Just prior to the time that he sold the business, our nation was in the process of building a network of super highways that connected the entire country. An entrepreneur by the name of Kemmons Wilson foresaw a need to build lodging for the millions of travelers that would ensue. His simple formula of building a motor hotel at the intersections of these super highways spawned 'Holiday Inns of America.'

The only practical way to provide air conditioning for these motor hotels (or 'motels' as they became known) was with the decentralized, energy conserving air conditioning system that Laube pioneered. This became the spark that ignited acceptance of the Incremental System™, for motels, hotels and all other types of multi-room buildings. The Incremental System™ gained national acceptance in Holiday Inns and hundreds of other hotels and motels across the country. Singer Company and other manufacturers who followed would be the beneficiary of Laube's foresight and innovation.

Future iterations of decentralized air conditioning included water-source heat pump systems, and Geo Thermal heat pump systems (branded ECC for Energy Conservation Air Conditioning). Today, the entire air conditioning industry accepts Laube's theory of the economic advantages of decentralization and energy conservation air conditioning. Unfortunately, like so many of his ilk, Herb never realized the fame and fortune he truly deserved.

A complex and fascinating person, Laube's powerful mind and personality swept many into his sphere and motivated my desire to succeed. He was far from a saint, having more than his share of idiosyncrasies as well as an abundant ego. On the other hand, I have never known a business leader who did not fit this profile.

My first encounter with this man came in 1956 when I was working for a manufacturer's representative in Syracuse, New York. We sold heating equipment (the market for commercial air conditioning was just beginning). Herb called, introduced himself, and then commenced to regale me with details of a unique new decentralized air conditioning system that he had developed called the Incremental System™.

It was intended, at that time, for existing multi-room buildings such as hotels, office buildings and apartment houses. He explained how it could be installed through the wall thus avoiding an expensive, space-consuming central system. He explained that central air conditioning systems consume valuable building space and have much higher owning and operating costs. I listened politely, but it seemed like a Mickey Mouse way to air condition a major building (I had been trained, as a mechanical engineer in the traditional central system method). Telling him that we were not interested, I hung up the phone and thought that would be the end of it.

Laube then called my boss Hal Walsh and accused me of "not having the intellectual curiosity or vision to travel 25 miles to his factory and investigate a potentially lucrative business opportunity."

Hal prevailed upon me and we traveled the 25 miles to visit Laube at his factory, which was housed in a run-down plant that the mayor of Auburn had given Herb for one dollar (International Harvester, tired of local union problems had abandoned the plant several years earlier). Laube greeted us in his big barn of an office and his voice echoed as he repeated the sales pitch – this time with pictures of buildings that had installed this 'revolutionary' system (in reality there weren't many).

On the way home, Hal Walsh asked me what I thought and I told him it still seemed like an unconventional approach for air conditioning major commercial structures, but he was the boss and so we signed up as a Remington representatives.

Little did I realize how this would *forever* affect my life.

Laube insisted upon intense training of his sales force of independent manufacturer's representatives. Our first meeting was in a basement hall of the YMCA building in Auburn, New York (there were no conference facilities at the factory). The small but dedicated group consisted of some of the best reps in the Eastern part of the country (it would be many years before Remington had a national sales force).

Herb Laube preached the 'gospel' of how the air conditioning industry – dominated by Carrier, Trane and York – got off on the wrong track when the commercial multi-room market emerged after WW II. They all adapted the central chiller which had been developed for buildings such as factories, theatres and auditoriums. He explained that "The only way to provide full-time comfort for the occupant of a multi-room building at the lowest owning and operating cost is to utilize a decentralized air conditioning system."

It was a powerful story and it proved to be true. Everyone in that room became disciples and went forth to preach the gospel of comfort, low first cost, and efficient operation. That small group would come to have a major impact on the entire air conditioning industry in years to come.

Six years later, I was hired by Remington as regional sales manager, becoming sales manager a few years after that. I took the job, mainly, because Remington doubled my salary to the incredible sum of $10,000 per year, but also there was a feeling that I would learn much from this brilliant man. The first thing I learned about was Laube's uncommon loyalty to his employees. Three days after starting work for Remington I had a grievous hunting accident and hung on the edge of death for several weeks.

The doctors told Laube that it was unlikely I would ever work again. Subsequently, Herb learned that my hospitalization insurance had lapsed because of changing jobs so he kept me on the payroll even though it was months before I returned to work. This kind of loyalty rarely exists in today's corporate world.

Carrier then merged with York Ice Machine Company. Herb told me that, "With every merger there is a sub-merge." Later, I came to fully understand this as Remington Air Conditioning Division was bought by Singer Company, then Snyder General, then McQuay International, and today, Daikin Air Conditioning – a Japanese company.

In Carrier's early days, Laube was more or less their head salesman. Carrier's operations were located in Newark, New Jersey, and Herb continued his life-long ambition of being a pilot. He bought a biplane called the 'Buhl Bull Pup' (aptly named for Herb's personality). He was flying down the Jersey coastline to visit his girlfriend Louise (later his wife), when he ran out of gas. Coasting down to a landing on the beach, Herb walked to a filling station, got a can of gas, and continued his trip. When Herb's boss learned of his exploit he warned Herb that "The management of Carrier advances men, not only based on their ability, but also based on their sound judgment – on and off the job." Laube promptly ignored the advice. So far as I know no one ever told Herb what to do.

Carrier moved their operation to Syracuse in 1937, taking over the defunct Franklin Motor Company's factory on Geddes Street (closed down during the depression). Laube moved to Syracuse and bought a home in the country nearby. By this time, he was Vice President of Research and Development.

During WW II, Carrier developed a device that played a major role for U.S. victory in the battle of the Atlantic. It was called "The Mark 10 Anti-Sub Missile Firing Device" – nicknamed the "Hedgehog." Testing was done on Laube's country property. The Hedgehog was responsible for sinking more than 300 enemy U-Boats during the latter part of WW II, thereby rendering Axis submarines ineffective death-traps.

Several years before this time Laube had bought a small, defunct, company called 'Remington Machine Works' (manufacturer of ammonia compressors) at a sheriffs tax sale for $1,200.What he got was a couple of partially complete ammonia compressors, but what he wanted was the name 'Remington.' Herb reasoned that the public would think it was a division of the industrial giant Remington Rand and he named his infant company "Remington Air Conditioning Division." Thus Laube laid the groundwork for establishing his own business.

When Carrier heard of Laube's venture, they asked him to stay and offered to buy his interest in Remington. President Cloud Wampler also dangled the prospect that Herb was in line for the future presidency of Carrier. Herb agreed to stay (afterall, even a man with his drive had to consider supporting a wife and three small children in difficult economic times). Laube continued to climb the ladder of success at Carrier becoming Vice President of Engineering.

He later bragged that, at one point, Willis Carrier actually worked for him. The fact of the matter was that Willis Carrier was happiest working in the research lab and he left the running of the business to others. One day Cloud Wampler said to Herb, "Be sure to keep the chief busy." Laube had the greatest respect for Willis Carrier, always referring to him by the beloved title of "The Chief." He also had a great respect for Cloud Wampler – for without his efforts there would be no Carrier Corporation. However, conflict developed between these strong minded men soon after the end of the war as America entered a new phase of its development.

Before WW II, the primary use of air conditioning was for centralized applications such as factories, theatres and auditoriums. When the war ended America was left with gigantic industrial capacity that had to be converted from government production of war machines to the private sector. Demand was great, the economy was booming, and Americans wanted goods and creature comforts.

A building boom ensued and those buildings, mostly offices, hotels, hospitals and other multi-room structures, needed air conditioning. Along with this, existing multi-room buildings had to add air conditioning in order to compete with the new structures. All of a sudden, Carrier had an entirely new market for their air conditioning products. They hired a

Syracuse consultant by the name of George W. Meek to develop new systems to be used for these multi-room structures.

Meek presented a study which included three primary systems, two of which were adaptations of chiller based central cooling plants, and a third system, which incorporated a modification of the window air conditioner. This third system consisted of through-wall air conditioners, similar in operation to window units but designed to heavy duty commercial standards, with components that would equal central plants in life and reliability.

Laube was taken with this through-wall system and urged Carrier to let him develop the products. Wampler, concerned that it would cannibalize chiller sales, killed the idea. At this point, Laube wrested the dormant, 'Remington Air Conditioning Division' back from Carrier and resigned to start his own business.

The primary goal of Laube's new company would be to develop what he would call the 'Incremental System™' - which was Meek's third proposal to Carrier. Thus, Remington started operation in 1948 renting factory space in Cortland, New York. Shortly after that, Maury Scwartz, then mayor of Auburn, offered Remington a defunct factory building for one dollar – very much the same as the mayor of Syracuse had done to attract Carrier to Syracuse in 1937.

I joined Remington in 1961, as regional sales manager, during a time of great financial difficulty (unknown to me). Laube had made a heavy investment in sales managers in order to set up a nationwide network of manufacturer's representatives. My region was the Northeast, which was the area of greatest growth potential.

The learning curve was fast and steep. I learned never to enter Herb's office without paper and pencil, in order to take notes of everything discussed, and also learned always to initial and date every piece of paper (years later as I write this book – the wisdom of his teaching comes to mind). Monday morning staff meetings were an institution. We learned, at these meetings, that alibis and excuses for not getting assignments done were simply not tolerated. Underneath Laube's hard crust was a soft heart and he disliked firing people, but he had a method that was equally effective. He would be on your case until you shaped up or shipped out.

Many shipped out.

Herb had an uncanny ability to boil things down to their essentials. He was a voracious reader and skimmed all periodicals associated with our industry. Since Remington operated on a tight budget, only one copy of these publications came to the office. Herb read them first, underlining a sentence here, a phrase there, and then passed it to his staff. Each of us would cross off our initials and pass to the next on the list. We all learned that by reading Laube's underlined sections, we could get the gist without reading the entire piece. Herb taught us that all data could usually be boiled down into five basic factors, principles, or reasons. Sometimes it would be necessary to expand to ten if it was an extremely complex subject. Why five or ten? Because a person has five fingers on each hand – which allows you to tick them off and more easily memorize the data.

Not all we learned from Herb was beneficial. He was the first to admit that he sacrificed family for the sake of business. His car could usually be seen at the office on Thanksgiving, Christmas, and most other holidays and he hardly ever took vacations. His heart and soul was on a quest to make his mark in the air conditioning industry, and to preach a gospel of energy conservation, elimination of polluting fossil fuels, development of renewable energy, conservation of natural resources, and elimination of waste. In other words, what we know today as the 'Greening of America.'

Laube's product philosophy was to build the highest quality equipment with no planned obsolescence. He said, "If your competitor wants to build a cheaper product, that's their business but never let a competitor make your decisions." On the other hand, if a competitor has a good idea, there is nothing wrong with copying it. That – he called – "design by analogy."

Herb's marketing strategy was 'The Golden Rule' – he who has the gold makes the rule. Find the person with the money and show them how to make or save money with your system, product or service and, if they are objective, you will make a sale. All commercial buying decisions are made (or should be made) for one of two reasons – hope of profit, or fear of loss of profit. Laube's service philosophy was "The favorable testimony of a satisfied user is *the* most powerful sales tool." A customer will seldom blame you for having product problems but they will always blame you for not taking care of them.

Some treasured Laube-isms:

Knowledge is power. **The acquisition of knowledge is a never-ending endeavor. The application of that knowledge is the main ingredient for success.**

Nothing is as powerful as an idea whose time has come. **The corollary is, no one wants to be first, but every one wants to be *among* the first.**

The KISS principle. **Keep It Simple Stupid. The corollary is 'the ultimate in sophistication is simplicity itself.' The best solution to any problem is the simplest.**

Never leave business for business. **Many businesses become successful, and then lose their way reaching out for more.**

What else does it change? **This sign, which hung in the center of Remington's engineering department, saved countless mistakes.**

The NIH syndrome **(Not Invented Here). Egotism and vanity has prevented many companies from profiting from the ideas of others.**
.
Don't procrastinate. **Many people will think of reasons why something should be done – then go on to think of potential problems, and end up doing nothing.**

Sometimes it's better to be lucky than smart. **Don't get over-confident. Your success may not always be the result of your genius.**

Herb Laube was the best writer and public speaker I have ever known and this talent was instrumental in his success. Communicative skills are at the core of most people's success. After all, what good are ideas if they can't be effectively communicated to others?

There is still ample opportunity in America's dynamic society for men like Herbert Laube to make their mark today, but to a certain extent, his kind is dying out. Those willing to sacrifice everything for an idea or principle are rare indeed. Who knows what drives such men. Rather than ponder this, it is better just to be thankful that there are such men who continue to keep this great country unique in the entire world.

There is no Substitute For
On the Job Training

Knowledge is power. From the neck down, your income is limited to whatever McDonald's is paying to flip hamburgers. From the neck up --- there is no limit to your earning power. Formal education is an integral part of obtaining knowledge, but, that said, the college diploma that you frame and hang on the wall has no more relevance to wisdom and success than the diploma that the Wizard of Oz gave to the scarecrow. Too often people think that a diploma guarantees a high-paying job when, in reality, it can be an opiate.

After graduating from school in 1951, I got a job in the engineering department of Solvay Process. The job turned out to be little more than being a draftsman. It became boring with little hope of advancement beyond the drafting board. One night on the way home from work I stopped at Sergeant, Webster, Crenshaw & Folley – the largest architectural firm in Syracuse at the time. Their business was booming because of the need for new schools. The baby boomers were coming of school age. A job was offered to me in their heating, ventilating, and air conditioning (HVAC) department.

Learning how to design HVAC systems was challenging, but it still meant being chained to a drafting board most of the time. However, I did get a chance to design one of the very first commercial air conditioning projects in Syracuse – Shopping Town in DeWitt. Manufacturers' representatives called on us regularly in order to get their products specified and that started to get me thinking of a career in engineering sales.

While on lunch break one day I stopped at Lennox Company on Midler Avenue – it was a manufacturer of furnaces and other heating equipment, making some of its products in Syracuse. By luck, Harold Yaisel, who was sales manager, was having a sandwich at his desk. In response to my query about becoming a sales engineer he said, "Son, a lot of people want to become a salesman because they see dapper guys with late model cars calling on them. Truth of the matter is, that unless you have a passion for sales, it's a tough business with long hours and a lot of traveling – but if you think you would like to try – I can probably line you up with our local manufacturers' rep."

Thus began my sales career.

Hal Walsh started in the heating business as a contractor sewing canvas jacketing over asbestos on steam pipes for institutional buildings such as hospitals and prisons. When Johns Manville invented and developed applied piping insulation it put him out of business overnight. At that point Walsh became a manufacturers' representative for heating equipment.

He hired me to help him apply and sell the equipment because he had no experience in the field of engineering sales. The commercial air conditioning market was just emerging. Walsh was not technically trained, but he was one of the best salesmen and the finest gentleman you could ever hope to know. During the early days of my sales training, when we made sales calls together, he would sit next to me and kick me below the table when I put my foot in my mouth. One of the lines we took on was Remington Air Conditioning which thrust us into the commercial air conditioning business. I attended sales meetings at Remington and heard Herb Laube preach the gospel of energy conservation air conditioning.

We were very successful selling Remington equipment and this, in turn, led me to accept an offer with Remington in 1961 as regional sales manager. Remington afforded my greatest on-the-job training experience. I learned how to motivate, manage, and mentor subordinates as well as the art of hiring and training salesmen. Team-building was an important curriculum and we learned that nothing can be accomplished in the field of management without the help and cooperation of others. Making mistakes is also an important ingredient of on-the-job training. My boss told me, "If you're not making mistakes, you're not advancing, but if you do make a mistake – own up to it so that the damage can be contained." This falls into the category of character. Herb Laube sold the business to Singer Company in 1966. He soon regretted it, but the damage was done and it was the beginning of the end for the Remington 'team.'

My resignation as sales manager of Remington was tendered on January 1, 1969, and Modular Comfort Systems, a new firm of manufacturers' representatives specializing in energy conservation air conditioning systems, started operation on April 1, 1969. Thus my on-the-job training and sales management career came full circle. Every job I had since graduating from school became a logical sequence for, what turned out to be, my final career as an entrepreneurial businessman.

However, on-the-job training has never ended.

Will you have 20 years' experience or one year's experience 20 times? This depends on whether you continue training in your chosen field, or drop the hammer in the middle of a swing when the whistle blows. Today, technology is advancing at such a rapid pace that if you rest on your laurels, the world will soon pass you by.

Ninety percent of all the technology utilized since man learned how to make fire has been developed within the past 100 years and has advanced exponentially since the turn of the 21st century. Continued education and on-the-job training is but a key stroke away on that computer that sits in your office, or on your lap. In the end-game – for any endeavor – success is preparedness combined with opportunity.

EPILOGUE PART 2

Call Your Shot

On a beautiful afternoon in Florida, a boatload of Haitian refugees somehow managed to sneak through the Coast Guard patrol boats, plying back and forth off the beaches of Miami and came within a couple hundred yards of a Causeway. Fifty desperate men, women, and children spilled overboard and scrambled onto the narrow spit of land beneath. There, they huddled, wet, cold and hungry – hoping against hope that they would be allowed to stay. This scenario plays out hundreds of times a year, along the Florida Coast and elsewhere on the borders of the greatest country in the world.

America still shines like a beacon of hope for those who dream of a better life. From the beginning of its time in history, our country has been populated by those, like the Haitian refugees, who risk all for the opportunity that only this nation provides. From the Pilgrims escaping oppression, to the Irish escaping famine, to the Jews escaping death in WW II, this country has always kept the door open and the beacon shining. No one ever expressed this credo better than Emma Lazarus in her famous poem, "Give me your tired, your poor, your huddled masses, yearning to breath free."

The opportunity for a better life, however, comes with a price. Every ethnic group has had to fight against hardship and discrimination in order to find their place in the sun .The early generations had to work hard, often in sweatshop conditions and often for meager wages. Their goals were always the same – to give their children a better life. They scrimped and saved, and sacrificed to educate the next generation. Like tempered steel, each generation emerged smarter, tough minded, not afraid to work for their dreams, not limited to their fathers' social status, and not afraid to fight in order to preserve their independence.

The entrepreneurial spirit was born in America. Go West young man, to open new territories, to create a new industry, and work far into the night, by candlelight, in order to invent electric light. Build the first automobile for the masses, or put the knowledge of the world on a micro-chip. America has created an atmosphere where the mind is not stifled, the soul is not oppressed, imagination is revered, and nothing is impossible. Success begins with the individual but is nurtured by the American dream.

A plaque hangs on the wall of my office, author unknown, which appeared in *Barons* magazine many years ago. Its prophetic wisdom has provided inspiration to me for lo these many years:

CALL YOUR SHOT

The reason most people don't get what they want out of life is because *they don't know what they want.*

They never completely define their objectives, even to themselves.

Is it any wonder that the wishful arrows they shoot in the general direction of the target, seldom make a bull's-eye?

It may sound ridiculous to some, but there is ample evidence to prove that a man can be pretty much what he wants to be – if he will decide what that is, and concentrate all his thoughts and actions on it.

A man's powers – often unrecognized – have a way of matching his dreams. He can't win, however, just by wishing. He must concentrate everything he has on reaching his goal *and give up everything that stands in his way.*

EPILOGUE PART THREE

After The Battle Is Won

Leon Danco, noted author of the book, *"Beyond Survival; A Guide for Business Owners and Their Families,"* said, "Company founders look upon retirement as something between euthanasia and castration." Harold Geneen, the former head of International Telephone and Telegraph (ITT) said, "If you keep working, you'll last longer. I'd hate to spend the rest of my life trying to outwit an 18" fish." On the other hand, Oliver Wendell Holmes said, "It is very grand to die in harness, but it is very pleasant to have the tight straps unbuckled and the heavy collar lifted from the head and shoulders."

A businessman who is used to traveling through life at 80 miles per hour cannot slam on the brakes and sit there with the engine idling – frustration is sure to follow. This syndrome is called, "the frustrated executive with nothing to exec." We see this happen often in our Florida community where we spend the winter season. Playing golf and sitting on the beach is not usually the formula for happiness for a person who has spent a career creating, motivating, and directing. Something has to fill the void, at least to a partial degree. Yes – there are exceptions, but the majority of us need a creative outlet for self-esteem and happiness in retirement. For me it has been a career in journalism, writing books, and racing cars among other things.

Reasonably good health is also an important part of the equation, and it becomes even more important to maintain a healthy mind and body as the aging process puts a strain on our faculties. First of all, I recommend easing into retirement if you have a flexible work schedule. Take it for a spin around the block before beginning the journey. Instead of slamming on the brakes – shift to a lower gear. For the last few years before full retirement, my partner and I rotated on a three-week cycle of work and partial retirement in the Florida sun.

At this juncture it is usually advisable to turn over control, at least partially, to your designated successor – in my case it was my sons. This not only tests the mettle of those you have designated to take over the reins, but it offsets the feeling of a rudderless ship for your employees. However, avoid the one-foot-in-the-stirrup and one-foot-on-the-ground situation indefinitely. This produces frustration for all involved.

Before your final curtain call - plan your "retirement career." I learned this trick from Herb Laube – as I learned almost everything else about business. Herb wrote a book, "How to Have Air Conditioning and Still be Comfortable," which was a takeoff on the foibles of the air conditioning industry. This book continues that theme, but on a light-hearted scale.

Many business leaders find pleasure and fulfillment in passing their considerable knowledge on to others – either by teaching, writing, lecturing, or consulting. On the other hand you might wish to pursue artistic talents long buried under the yoke of a career. Remember, Grandma Moses began painting at the age of eighty.

The most important investment you will make, however, is to insure that your retirement is a happy and healthy time, and not a train wreck. Unfortunately, the latter is true for the many of us whose business career *was* their life. How many times have we seen successful people retire and succumb to depression, ill-health, or just plain boredom?

What follows is a road map for the golden years:

When someone asked William F. Buckley how he felt, during his later years, his usual reply was –"decomposing – but other than that fine." Of course he was right – we all start decomposing from the time of our birth. Our cells are constantly dying to be replaced with new. Every cell in our body is replaced within seven years. Eventually, tissue, cartilage, and bone break down.

The process can be controlled and slowed, however, by diet, exercise and good health habits augmented by modern wonder drugs, vitamins and dietary supplements. Each generation is living longer, healthier, active lives. The president of our condominium association in Florida is 91 years young at this writing, and his mind is as sharp as a tack.

Our senior years can be trying, or a time of happiness and fulfillment. Remember that life is a journey and not a destination. In order to enjoy what I consider to be the best part of the journey – it will be necessary to address the four functions of longevity:

THE BODY – As we age, the cartilage that cushions and lubricates our joints deteriorates and arthritis can set in. Tendons become weak and often rupture; bones become brittle and lose density. Bodybuilding can offset this by strengthening the muscles that activate the joints and by taking pressure off the cartilage, tendons, and bones. Bodybuilding also helps control the flab that builds around the middle. The current generation does bodybuilding to stay fit and attract the opposite sex – we do it to stay comfortable and remain active.

Vitamins and dietary supplements can restore calcium to our bones, rebuild cartilage, and enhance blood flow. Flax seed or fish oil does wonders for digestion and there are myriad other balms for the body to augment what nature gradually takes away.

Next in line comes aerobic exercising to elevate the heartbeat above normal for at least 15 minutes a day four or five days a week. My wife and her lady friends walk around our complex almost every day. This not only satisfies aerobics, but it is also an excellent way to keep up on the latest neighborhood gossip. My routine is to ride the bicycle, work out at the gym, and (weather permitting) swim in the ocean, lake or pool.

THE MIND – The mind is much like a muscle – if you do not exercise it regularly, it will atrophy. There is ample scientific evidence that mental exercising can be a major factor in offsetting Alzheimer's disease as well as other forms of dementia.

There are a raft of activities that keep the mind sharp including bridge, crossword puzzles, word games such as Scrabble (my favorite), and a variety of computer games. Speaking of computers – many of my generation have avoided the electronic marvel that is changing the way the world communicates. One day, newspapers, magazines, books, music, (snail) mail, and even television will be drastically changed because of the computer. The time to enter into the brave new electronic world is now. Ask your grandchildren to teach you – they know better than anyone.

THE IMMUNE SYSTEM – A bout with cancer taught me the value of the immune system – our defense mechanism that protects us against everything from the common cold to cancer, and many other maladies that attack our bodies. The immune system can break down from a variety of factors including stress, poor diet, lack of exercise, depression, and just plain unhappiness. After the career battle is won, you must face one more challenge – and that is maintaining happiness and healthiness in retirement.

THE SPIRIT – PMA (positive mental attitude) is absolutely essential for a long and fruitful life. Aging is mostly a state of mind. Whether you think you are old, or you think you are not – you're right! My idol, my hero, my role model was octogenarian Paul Newman – movie actor, entrepreneur, philanthropist (creator of the Hole-in-the-Wall Gang for young terminal cancer victims), and team owner of Newman-Hass racing. Paul drove his last race just after the turn of the 21st century – the 24 hours of Daytona (one of the longest and most grueling of all venues) piloting car number 79 (his age at the time). He did a damn fine job.

My race car number is 69 – which is the year I started. Racing has been the greatest challenge of my lifetime – it brings together all the factors of mental and physical acuity – and most importantly – exercises my passion for life.

www.ingramcontent.com/pod-product-compliance
Lightning Source LLC
Chambersburg PA
CBHW030856180526
45163CB00004B/1602